Throughout this book, Kathy Longo offers a wealth manager's entrepreneurial perspective on moving beyond the numbers. Her client stories and insights provide essential understanding to her approach in serving clients. An engaging must-read for clients and prospective clients of Flourish Wealth Management.

Sarah Asebedo, PhD, CFP®

Assistant Professor, Texas Tech University;

President, Financial Therapy Association

This is a wise and wonderful guidebook for weaving together your values and your money to flourish and live a rich life—regardless what life throws at you.

Use this book to prepare for important, yet sometimes difficult, money conversations with your family and your advisors.

Susan Bradley, CFP® , CeFT®

Founder, Sudden Money Institute

Kathy Longo offers us her industry wisdom and experience in a practical yet thought-provoking book. She challenges our traditional silo-mentality thinking about financial planning and offers us a more holistic and interconnected approach to wealth management. Now, we all have the ability to flourish financially.

Jane Dailey

Co-owner/founder, Hollywood Fashion Tape, Inc.

In Flourish Financially, *Kathy Longo provides a helpful template for starting conversations about money and money values. I've always respected Kathy's high integrity in the field of financial planning and I'm pleased to support her first book. Based on my experience working with couples and individuals who need to have conversations about money, I believe reading this book will help people to have more productive money conversations, resulting in a more balanced money life.*

Ruth Hayden

Nationally recognized financial consultant;
educator and author based out of St. Paul, Minnesota

Money is the last great taboo subject. Even within families, where money decisions can have significant long-term impact on everyone in the household. In her book, Kathy provides the valuable tools necessary to understand our own personal money stories, break down the walls of silence, and finally facilitate the meaningful money conversations necessary for families to flourish financially.

Michael Kitces

Director of Financial Planning at Pinnacle Advisory Group;
publisher of Nerd's Eye View financial planning industry blog

flourish financially

flourish financially

VALUES, TRANSITIONS, & **BIG CONVERSATIONS**

Kathy Longo, CFP®

Published by Advantage, Charleston, South Carolina.
Member of Advantage Media Group.

ADVANTAGE is a registered trademark, and the Advantage colophon is a trademark of Advantage Media Group, Inc.

Printed in the United States of America.

10 9 8 7 6 5 4 3 2 1

ISBN: 978-1-59932-932-1
LCCN: 2018950990

Cover design by Melanie Cloth.
Layout design by Carly Blake.

This publication is designed to provide accurate and authoritative information in regard to the subject matter covered. It is sold with the understanding that the publisher is not engaged in rendering legal, accounting, or other professional services. If legal advice or other expert assistance is required, the services of a competent professional person should be sought.

Advantage Media Group is proud to be a part of the Tree Neutral® program. Tree Neutral offsets the number of trees consumed in the production and printing of this book by taking proactive steps such as planting trees in direct proportion to the number of trees used to print books. To learn more about Tree Neutral, please visit **www.treeneutral.com**.

Advantage Media Group is a publisher of business, self-improvement, and professional development books and online learning. We help entrepreneurs, business leaders, and professionals share their Stories, Passion, and Knowledge to help others Learn & Grow. Do you have a manuscript or book idea that you would like us to consider for publishing? Please visit **advantagefamily.com** or call **1.866.775.1696**.

To my children, Madeline, Fernando, and Grace.
To my husband, Jay.
And to my parents, Bob and Diane.

TABLE OF CONTENTS

Foreword

What does it mean to live a rich life—literally and figuratively?

The first part of this question is one that the financial services industry has long focused on. Helping individuals identify the ways in which their hard-earned money should be invested has been the staple of financial advice. For fiduciary-oriented financial advisors who practice true wealth management, their advice could expand to include retirement needs analyses, risk management assessments, estate planning guidance, and keeping an eye on tax-minimization.

If your eyes are glazing over reading the above paragraph, you are not alone. For most of us, having the technical aspects of our personal finances in order is a necessary—but not sufficient—condition for feeling true calm, confidence, and clarity around our money.

That's because money so often is about far more than mere dollars and cents. In a work environment, money can signify how much you are appreciated by your employer or how you "stack up" against your peers in the office or in your industry. On the home front, money can be a tool for freedom—one that gives you a voice and a choice to live the life that makes your heart sing. Or, conversely, money can be a tool to control and dominate another. In a social setting, money can be a gigantic pink elephant standing in the middle of the restaurant table when it comes time to pay the check, or when deciding with friends which social events to attend.

In modern society it feels like there are very few topics that are inappropriate for the proverbial dinner table. Between the divisive 2016 presidential election to the #MeToo movement of 2018, topics such as politics and sex have been put squarely at the center of media coverage and social discourse. But the topic of money—how much each of us earns, has, spends, wants—remains shrouded in societal secrecy.

That's a shame, because it's simply not possible to live a rich life figuratively if you are feeling unspoken or unacknowledged stress around your finances. All too often those stresses occur in some of our most intimate relationships—with our spouse, our parents, our children, our siblings, and our friends. Figuring out how to navigate these tricky money conversations is a skill that for far too long has not been taught.

Enter *Flourish Financially*.

In this delightful book, wealth manager Kathy Longo shows us how to have the necessary money conversations with the key people in our lives. Drawing on her more than two decades of experience advising individuals and families, Kathy helps readers understand what emotions drive their own financial decisions. She also identifies the crucial types of life transitions that can impact financial planning and require authentic—potentially uncomfortable—conversations. And most important of all, she gives specific guidance on how to handle a wide range of potentially tricky conversations. Read this gem of a book and prepare to enjoy your own rich life and Flourish Financially.

Manisha Thakor, CFA, CFP®

VP, Financial Education at Brighton Jones

Introduction

In 2013, my client Jeff[1] was obviously worn down by his job. Every time Jeff and I met to review his financial plan, I'd ask about how various aspects of his life were going and would see him physically change. His shoulders would slump, his voice would soften, and he would lose his color. Jeff was married and had two kids who were headed to college in the next few years. At the time, I was a minority partner in a large financial planning firm. I was doing well helping people plan for their futures, but something was missing for me. One day, I asked Jeff if there was something that he'd rather be doing. He perked up, color came back into his face, and he told me that he'd always dreamed of running his own business. The idea of taking the steps to do it was daunting. Jeff was earning a nice salary with a great benefits package and didn't want to sacrifice this financial security for the unknown. That was his biggest hurdle.

Over time, Jeff and I worked out a plan that would allow him to accumulate the assets he needed to feel comfortable going out on his own. We also modeled various scenarios that showed what starting a new business would look like for him financially, and we discussed a fallback idea—plan B—in case his business failed. In Jeff's case, plan B would give him a few years to work on his business and, if it didn't

---

1   Names of clients and some details have been changed to protect their identity.

work out, he would begin looking for work with a large company.

As I continued working with Jeff and saw how energized he was by making plans to live out his dream, I noticed something: I saw myself in him. His entrepreneurial spirit and his yearning to do something else really struck a chord with me. I heard myself giving advice to Jeff about how we need to make sure our work is meaningful because it's such a big part of us and how it's crucial to examine the financial barriers keeping us from living our dreams. That's when I realized I needed to take my own advice.

I'd always been interested in starting my own business. When I started thinking about what had been holding me back from doing it for so many years, I again saw myself in Jeff. I was afraid to go out on my own because I didn't want to forgo a good salary and a comfortable lifestyle. To start my own business, I had to break free of the same barriers Jeff had to.

I worked through my plan to start a business the same way I had helped Jeff work through his. I mapped out what it would look like if I took a risk and became a new business owner. I looked at what would need to happen, both personally and financially, to make that happen. Then I came up with my plan B, my fallback plan. At the time, I had a non-solicit agreement with my firm. I didn't know if any of my clients would follow. So for me, the worst thing that could happen was that clients wouldn't follow me, I wouldn't attract new clients, and I'd have to go back to working for another company. I knew I didn't want to do that, but I also knew that I *could* do it. The other thing I had to do was talk to my family about changing some of their spending habits. I had to have conversations with my husband and my three kids about our budgets, how they would change, and why.

Financial management came to me via a circuitous route. I went to Purdue University to study economics. One semester, I accidentally discovered financial planning. A classmate recommended a personal finance class, and when I took it, I realized I loved everything about it. It had the numbers, but it also talked about how to plan for your kids' education, what happens when you die, and what happens if you don't make plans for your assets. I was hooked, so I switched majors. At the time, financial planning was a new major. Only two dozen schools offered this degree. Today, about one hundred and thirty schools offer degrees in financial planning, including doctorate programs in this field. Even though financial planning was a new major at the time, the idea of using my knowledge to help other people discover their goals and what is important to them was incredibly appealing to me.

After I switched majors, I enrolled in several communication and psychology classes, which allowed me to better understand the emotional factors that drive our financial decisions. Financial planners work with people when they're going through their most exhilarating and devastating life transitions—marriage, divorce, birth, death—and I wanted to help people gain clarity on their values as well as their goals to successfully prepare and navigate through all of these life events.

After graduation, I worked for Carol Pankros. Carol owned a wealth management firm in Palatine, Illinois, and was one of the few women in the industry at that time. Carol was a fiduciary, so she was committed to always acting in her clients' best interests. We met at a conference hosted by Purdue University, hit it off, and I became Carol's first employee, and she my mentor.

When Carol hired me, she couldn't quite afford me. I made about $18,000 a year, and she shared my time with another financial planner until she could pay me for full-time work. In the meantime, I watched Carol grow her business and be involved in the financial planning professional community while also raising a family. That planted the seed that I could have it all and own my own firm one day.

In 2014 my passion for helping people, my commitment to taking the advice I give my own clients, and the confidence Carol's inspiration instilled in me came together in such a way that I was able to launch Flourish Wealth Management, an independent wealth management firm focused on helping clients understand their money history, grow comfortable with their money values, gain confidence in having conversations about money, and create the financial freedom to live the life of their dreams.

My vision was to create a nimble firm that would adapt to every client's needs. I wanted to be more hands-on. I wanted to be more involved in the relationship with my clients, and I wanted to tune into the pulse of each client. I desired to create a boutique wealth management experience that had the technology, tools, resources, and team that would allow us to provide a more customized approach to each client. In addition, many financial planners overlook the psychological elements that drive financial decisions. With Flourish, I wanted to develop a culture and process that would fully incorporate those important considerations into my clients' financial goals.

When I talk about Flourish, I like to introduce the Wheel of Life, which represents the nine core areas where we typically spend our time: finances, family, health, leisure, learning, inner growth, home, community, and work.[2] Created by an organization called Money Quotient, this is one of the financial planning tools we use to help us get to the heart of our clients' values and priorities, establish meaningful financial and life goals, and create an effective and inspiring decision-making framework. To me, flourishing is when a person feels connected and aligned to these areas of their personal and financial

---

2   "The Wheel of Life," Money Quotient, Inc., moneyquotient.org.

life, giving them a sense of satisfaction. It is about being aware of one's values and priorities and making financial choices in each area of life that align with and support those values and priorities. The outcome is a sense of satisfaction, personal well-being, and intrinsic reward. Once I launched Flourish Wealth Management, I realized I was finally becoming a living example of the advice I give my clients. I was connected and aligned in each of the nine areas represented by the Wheel of Life. The idea of flourishing had become self-fulfilling.

My husband, Jay Pluimer, and I have three kids: Madeline (Maddy), age twenty-one; Fernando, age twelve; and Grace, age twelve. Before we could officially move into the Flourish Wealth Management office space, our dining room was overtaken with Flourish material. New stationery, office supplies, phone and computer equipment, and documents spilled over the table and the floor. We were so excited to transition into our official office space that all the kids helped with the move. They unpacked supply boxes, vacuumed the carpet, and stocked pencils, pens, and staplers. Maddy quickly signed up to organize the new kitchen and assist with paperwork. Fernando and Grace pretended to answer the phone by saying, "Flourish Wealth Management, how can I help you?" In addition to having my kids involved in the business, Jay is our director of investments. Jay and I met at an investment class and he initially pursued me with a combination of economic updates and love notes (I much preferred the notes!), cementing our personal connection with a shared passion for helping others through finances.

It's incredibly exciting to have my family involved in Flourish. However, I never would have started Flourish if I hadn't taken the time to consider the possibilities for my life. There's such great happiness that comes out of being connected to your true self versus letting other factors in your life limit you. It's empowering, it's freeing, and it makes a difference in every aspect of your life. Just the other day, Jay looked at me, smiled, and said, "I know you're busier than ever, but I've also never seen you happier."

Since opening Flourish in 2014, we've added staff, expanded our office space, and seen steady growth, particularly among our female clients in transition, who find our firm to help them with divorce, the death of a spouse, or inheritance. Based in part on our expertise in these areas, women in transition represent about 40 percent of our clientele. Early in 2017, we hit $100 million of assets under management. It was a celebratory moment, but it wasn't the most notable moment in Flourish's history. Every time our team has grown—we are now at six team members—I was reminded that Flourish is about more than a number. It's about an appreciation for the impact we have on our team and our clients.

Clients tell me again and again that they appreciate the Flourish team because we support them during each of life's key moments, whether it's a heart attack, a marriage, or retirement. For me, these comments validate that Flourish has become a trusted advisor for clients seeking personal counsel during life's largest transitions. This is why Advisory HQ ranked Flourish as one of the top ten advisory firms in Minnesota for the third consecutive year in 2018.[3]

Whether it's our family, our team members, or our clients, we want to help everyone flourish. And in order for everyone to flourish, uncomfortable conversations about money and life need to happen. After working in financial planning for more than twenty-five years, I've noticed that there's a deep-rooted resistance in our culture to talk about money. Talking about money requires a willingness to be vulnerable and most people are not confident in their money

---

3   Advisory HQ, "2018 Ranking of the Top Financial Advisors in Minneapolis, St. Paul, and Edina (Minnesota)" (2018): https://www.advisoryhq.com/articles/top-rated-financial-advisors-in-minnesota/.

choices. They're embarrassed about making poor choices or not having the know-how to make good ones. This is unfortunate for many reasons. Chief among them is the fact that money is a source of stress for most people. A 2017 PricewaterhouseCoopers (PwC) Employee Financial Wellness Survey, which tracks the financial and retirement well-being of US working adults, showed that 53 percent of all employees are stressed about their finances.[4] Over half of this country's largest source of stress is money, yet for most of us, it's the hardest thing to talk about. An American Express study found that 91 percent of couples find reasons to avoid talking about finances and only 43 percent discussed money before marriage.[5] A UK study reported that 44 percent of people don't feel comfortable managing their own money.[6] It also showed that 39 percent of parents don't feel confident talking about money with their kids. We are not honest with ourselves about money and we avoid talking about it with our spouses, children, and siblings.

In this book, I will teach you how to have necessary and sometimes uncomfortable money conversations with the key people in your life so you can make the best financial decisions for yourself and your family. When you finish *Flourish Financially*, you will understand the emotions that drive your own financial decisions, understand how crucial life transitions impact financial planning, and feel comfortable having necessary financial conversations with the key people in your life. We all want to feel good about our financial decisions

---

4 PWC, Financial Stress and the Bottom Line, special report, https://www.pwc.com/us/en/industries/private-company-services/library/financial-well-being-retirement-survey.html.

5 American Express, "Money Trumps Children and In-Laws as Source of Relationship Stress According to American Express Spending & Savings Tracker," press release, http://about.americanexpress.com/news/pr/2010/mtc.aspx.

6 The Money Advice Service, "Just 40% of Young people Are Taught Money Management," press release, https://www.moneyadviceservice.org.uk/en/corporate/press-release-just-40-of-young-people-are-taught-money-management.

because they affect every aspect of our life. I can help you have the meaningful and productive conversations that will allow you to make good financial decisions. Let's make today a day to flourish.

Kathy Longo

PART 1
Values

W hen we first meet with clients at Flourish Wealth Management, we often introduce them to the Wheel of Life, a representation of the nine areas of life where we spend most of our time.

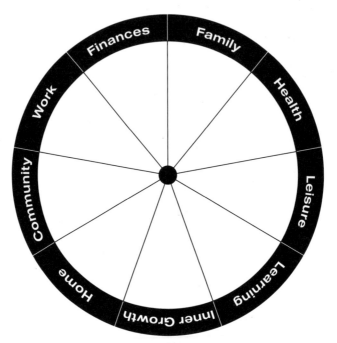

TO USE THE WHEEL OF LIFE[7] ...

- Place a dot on each spoke that indicates your level of satisfaction in that particular facet of life. Use a scale of zero to ten with zero at the center of the circle and ten at the rim. A zero indicates no satisfaction, and a ten indicates the highest degree of satisfaction.

- Now draw a line to connect the dots and create your life wheel.

---

7   "The Wheel of Life," Money Quotient, Inc., moneyquotient.org.

- Is your life wheel round or does it show flat spots? Is it deflated or is it full? What does this exercise tell you about your life? How balanced is your life? Are there areas of your life that need attention? In what facets would you like to experience more satisfaction?

While we realize that each of the nine elements that make up the Wheel of Life will never be completely in balance, it's important to understand that everything is interconnected. Finance does not exist in a silo, nor does health, community, or family. The Wheel of Life helps us realize that when one area of the wheel is unsatisfying, it bleeds into and affects other areas of the wheel. For example, if you have a health issue, the focus needed to address that issue might change your work situation. Maybe you have to think differently about your work environment or pull back on your hours, which then interplays with your finances. This, in turn, might affect your family. The Wheel of Life is an effective way to assess how you currently feel about each of these areas and how everything is interconnected. The idea behind the Wheel of Life is to get a snapshot of how satisfied clients are in every aspect of their lives while introducing the critical concept that each area of our life is connected. When used effectively, the Wheel of Life helps you clearly identify your current life satisfaction while visually acknowledging the aspects of your life that need more attention. The goal is to find a comfortable balance across each category to live a more satisfying life.

Right before I started Flourish, I ranked my work satisfaction as low and my desire for inner growth as high. From there, I had to assess what changes would improve my work situation. I had to focus on new goals and understand what those new goals would mean for every other piece of the wheel. That decision, of course, took sacrifice, but you can better assess where you're headed when you know where you currently are.

Part 1 of *Flourish Financially* is dedicated to values, because if you don't know your values, if you don't know what you want from your life, you can't set the financial goals you need to get those things. If you really want to focus on inner growth, that might mean you need to work less, which will affect your finances. If you want to focus on a career change, that will affect your finances. Finance is not a silo. It's an interconnected piece of your life. It affects everything and everything affects it.

Before you have the important conversations you need to have to reach your goals, you need to understand your values, your partner's values, your money history, and how your gender might play a role in your financial picture.

By the end of part 1 of this book, you will have a familiarity with your own values and your own money history that will allow you to flourish.

CHAPTER 1

Tell it Like it Is: Realizing Your Money Story

What Are Your Values?

When I was in seventh grade, I went shopping with a friend and her brother. They were from an affluent family and encouraged me to buy a pair of Guess jeans even though the Guess jeans were much more expensive than anything my family normally bought. Since fifth grade, I'd been earning my own money as the most-sought-after neighborhood babysitter, so I had enough money to buy the jeans. I was proud of my purchase until I brought the jeans home. My mom took one look at the price tag and made it clear that she thought I had paid way too much for them. I immediately felt ashamed. I took the jeans back, but the memory of them remains.

We All Have a Money Story

The reason the story of the Guess jeans still resonates with me is that it's part of my money story. Your money story is the history of financial decisions and financial influences that define how you view finance today. Your money story represents the emotional attachment you have to money that affects how you spend and save.

As an adult, I continue to mirror behaviors outlined in the Guess jeans story. I make my own money because I value financial independence, and I buy designer brands for the allure of them and also for their fashion. However, the Guess jeans experience taught me to be very conscious of the relationship between value and price. This helps me selectively choose when to buy a more expensive designer brand, based on whether it makes sense for me financially and emotionally. For example, I'll buy higher priced designer purses but can't justify paying a premium price for shoes. Shoes get beat up, especially in Minnesota winters. So for me, the investment doesn't make sense.

While your money story might be affected by bigger life transitions such as an inheritance or a job loss, more benign experiences like my Guess jeans one also affect your money story. Money stories are much more deeply rooted within a person's psyche than a single event that occurs in adult life. The Guess jeans incident is just one part of my money story.

MY MONEY STORY

If Guess taught me how to spend, my grandfather taught me how to save. When I was sixteen, I worked for Marshall Field's. It was my first W-2-type job. Not long after I started work, my grandfather said, "If you save money into an IRA, I will match whatever you put in."

My grandpa loved chatting about money. He worked for a utility line, but he was frugal and loved talking about his ability to save. This was taboo in my family where money wasn't discussed much.

My parents were very hardworking, a value they instilled in myself and my younger sister. My dad worked for a county highway transportation department in Illinois until retirement and walked away with a nice pension. To earn extra money for our family, my dad also had a job each Saturday working at a mansion, taking care of the home maintenance. My mom worked for several different companies. She was a hard worker but a little bit of a dreamer. Dad was the financially responsible one. Every week, Dad would sit down, look at everything we had spent, and come up with our budget for the rest of the month. I remember understanding that this was very serious work.

My parents paid to put me and my sister through Catholic school, but they had to make sacrifices in other areas to do it. So even though Dad would have preferred newer cars, he drove around in beaters. When I was a teenager, I would ask him to drop me off a block away from school so my friends wouldn't see his latest cost-saving vehicle. The floor on the passenger side of one of the cars was missing! Although Dad put some sort of board over the hole to make it safe, it was a questionable repair. Now that my dad is retired and in his seventies, he constantly replaces his cars, which are always new. Being a financial planner, I told him to hold on to his cars for longer, but after driving beaters around for years so we could go to school, he says he deserves to drive what he wants.

When I chose an out-of-state college, my parents took a loan from my grandpa to pay for it. This struck me as odd because I knew they didn't like my grandfather's readiness to talk about money. The loan caused tension in the house because my parents didn't want to talk about money, but my grandpa did, and the loan tied them together financially. My grandpa also had his opinions about how my parents should spend their money, which they didn't like either.

This brings me to the four specific incidences from my money story that have framed my views on spending and saving: (1) buying and then returning the Guess jeans (spending), (2) watching my dad track every dollar that went into and out of the house (spending), (3) investing in an IRA with my grandpa (saving), and (4) watching what happened when my parents took a loan from my grandpa (lending).

HOW MY MONEY STORY INFLUENCES MY FINANCIAL DECISIONS

My husband, Jay, knows more than anyone how much my money story has influenced my spending and savings decisions as an adult. I spend as my father does—I track everything that goes in and out of the house—and I save as my grandfather did, and talk about money often; I've even worked to inspire savers for the future by initiating money conversations with my children. I am fairly conservative; I like knowing that I have enough reserves to maintain my financial stability and independence.

No matter what your money story is, it will affect how you spend, save, and invest. By understanding your own money story, you can recognize the emotional components that drive each of your financial decisions.

Understand How Emotions Affect Your Money Story

Once I heard a podcast about Fermi's Paradox, which states that there is an enormous probability that we are completely alone in the universe. The journalist explaining the theory, David Kestenbaum, was also a particle physicist. He said he felt really sad every time he thought of Fermi's Paradox. His perspective was that "if we are alone … completely alone in the universe, then that means … this is it. There is nothing else out there that we can learn from or experience beyond what we, as human beings, can create."[8]

Thinking about Fermi's Paradox from the Kestenbaum's perspective is depressing but, if you think of it another way—that if we are 100 percent alone in the universe we can explore, chart, and amass great knowledge of this inconceivable giant space called the universe—it's not sad at all. In fact, it's exciting, a little scary, and an enormous responsibility.

All of us view our money story the way Kestenbaum and I view Fermi's Paradox: differently. How we perceive success, happiness, finance, and the experiences that shape us influences how we spend and save money. Understanding your money story and your emotions about money can remove some of the barriers that get in the way of allowing you to make level-headed financial decisions. You will always have emotions surrounding money, but if you can separate the emotional from the rational, you'll more clearly identify your true goals and make better financial decisions.

After examining my own money story, I understood that many of my financial decisions are driven by fear and responsibility. I fear that I will lose my financial independence and stability and feel responsible for making sure that doesn't happen. Fear and responsibility are two of the four most common emotions that drive financial decisions. The other two are excitement and sadness.

FEAR

The choices that we make about money are closely tied to fear. Fear is what stifles our ability to consider the long term. It can paralyze us to move forward, and it can cloud our judgment and cause us to make decisions out of perceived necessity rather than choice.

---

8   Ira Glass, David Kestenbaum, Stephanie Foo, "Fermi's Paradox," May 19, 2017, in *This American Life*, produced by Ira Glass, podcast, MP3 audio, 47:00, https://www.thisamericanlife.org/617/fermis-paradox.

People who enjoy watching their savings accumulate might have a fear of losing money. Therefore, they might forgo spending money on things that could bring them joy and knowledge, such as travel, dinners with friends and loved ones, or tickets to a concert. This fear might also stifle their ability to fulfill their long-term financial needs. While saving is a vital component of any long-term financial plan, it alone cannot satisfy most retirement needs. Effectively funding college tuition, paying for medical expenses, planning for retirement, and outpacing inflation typically requires some sort of investment strategy that offers more returns than savings alone.

While too much fear can prevent people from making wise financial decisions, a *lack* of fear can do the same. The excitement of investing in stocks and seeing the potential of what a dollar can do is intoxicating to some people. Their lack of fear of losing can also create money challenges that could hinder future financial security. Taking on too much risk can bring great wealth very quickly, but in some cases, the higher you climb the farther you fall.

CLIENT STORY
Facing Fears

Fear affects our money stories in interesting ways. My client Betty divorced when she was in her early forties, and when she came to me she was in her late sixties, retired, and had five grown kids, several of whom were struggling to take responsibility for their own finances. Betty had resources to support her retirement, but her kids continuously asked for large amounts of money. Betty felt that each of her kids should be treated equally, which meant that if she gave one of them money she would give the same amount to the other four. Even though she knew their requests could affect her long-term future, she couldn't say no. She feared that saying no would negatively impact her relationship with her children. Betty's approach to giving was driven by fear rather than joy. Eventually, she created a team to help her respond to each child's request by enlisting the help of her nephew (who was an attorney) to serve as a trustee of her assets. We worked together to explain to the kids that Betty had to reduce her giving to protect her long-term plan.

RESPONSIBILITY

The responsibility people feel for their finances can shift when they come into a large amount of money. This change can prevent them from making financial decisions or cause them to make unwise financial decisions. Other times, new wealth gives people the freedom to finally do what they've always wanted to do.

My client Lynn lost her father when she was young, which forced her mom to get a job. The job wasn't enough to pay the bills, so Lynn and her family went on food stamps and frequently received help from the local church. Later in life, Lynn married a man who, during their marriage, became wealthy from several business deals. Lynn's husband exerted tight control over their money. Lynn was the household CEO, and her husband would give her a weekly budget to manage household spending. Lynn resented her husband controlling their finances, giving her an envelope with a set amount of cash to cover groceries and other basic expenses but not giving her access to the checking account, and she was disappointed that she couldn't use some of the money to help others. Eventually, Lynn divorced her husband. With her half of the assets, she helped fund a charity that supported food banks. Because of Lynn's money history, she felt a responsibility to help others with her wealth and used the money she came into to finally accomplish what she wanted to do with her money.

EXCITEMENT

We all get excited about different things. Money and finances are no exception. When money begins to accumulate and you have expendable income, there are several things that can be done with it: you can save it, spend it, share it, or invest it. The responsible thing would be to craft a plan that incorporates all four, although that is not always what happens. Sometimes, excitement causes us to make poor financial decisions.

Some people get excited by the prospect of spending money and end up overspending. They don't just overspend on frivolous purchases; they sometimes overspend on seemingly practical invest-ments. Some may compromise their retirement by paying for a high-priced college for their kids because they feel they have the money now to do so. They feel that, somehow, someday, they will find a way to pay for retirement.

While excitement causes some to overspend, it causes others to over-save. Some people love watching their hard-earned dollars accumulate and grow. To them, this growth is more satisfying and rewarding than spending money. However this, too, can lead to poor financial choices.

CLIENT STORY
Meeting Halfway

I worked with a couple who progressed well in saving for their retirement. The husband's goal was to save $4 million, and he was extremely excited about watching his savings grow. He looked at his account values daily. I'm a financial planner and even I don't look at my accounts that frequently. The wife said he was obsessed with saving, which strained their relationship. Even though their mortgage was paid off and they had few expenses, the husband constantly presented ways to cut expenses and save more. The wife, on the other hand, wanted to travel and enjoy spending time together. The wife's money story involved her dad passing away shortly after he retired. That experience influenced her desire to enjoy life with her husband in case either ran into health problems that would affect their retirement. Her husband was excited about saving and, hence, he could not understand why her goals were all about living for the day.

While 44 percent of people feel more in control of their lives when they feel in control of their money situation, this couple illustrates why we need to strike a balance between our excitement for saving, spending, and enjoying life.[9] It took a while, but once this woman shared her money story with her husband, we found a middle ground where the husband was willing to spend more money to do the things she wanted to do.

---

9   The Money Advice Service, "Only a Fifth of UK Population Have a Money Mate Says New Survey," press release, Aug. 25, 2011, https://www.moneyadviceservice.org.uk/en/corporate/survey.

SADNESS

Money can cause a lot of excitement, but it can also cause a lot of sadness. The two main reasons people divorce are infidelity and disagreements over money.[10]

According to Utah State University researcher Jeffrey Dew, "Couples with consumer debt tend to fight more ... They are more stressed about their money, and some research that I have seen even shows that consumer debt is associated with divorce."[11]

And if couples aren't divorcing over money, they're fighting about it. A Yahoo! and *Fitness* magazine study showed that couples fight more about money than chores, kids, or sex.[12]

Not only is money the cause of many breakups, it's also the cause of many deaths. Research has shown that stress over money can lead to symptoms of depression and posttraumatic stress disorder (PTSD).[13] Issues surrounding money can make us sad, lonely, and helpless. They can also lead to suicide. The unfortunate pattern here is that money can be the catalyst for some of our most difficult struggles.

Sadness due to money problems can be debilitating. It can prevent individuals from making any decisions whatsoever about their financial future. Grief can also cause people to make illogical financial decisions. Sadness frequently affects financial decisions during difficult life transitions such as divorce or death. During a divorce, one or both parties might be so sad about the dissolution of

---

10   Shellie Warren, "10 Most Common Reasons for Divorce," Marriage. com, (January 31, 2018): https://www.marriage.com/advice/ divorce/10-most-common-reasons-for-divorce/.

11   Mark Bradshaw, "Love, Marriage and Financial Infidelity,' ABC Tulsa, (February 14, 2011): http://ktul.com/archive/love-marriage-and-financial-infidelity.

12   Loren Berlin, "Financial Advice for Couples to Avoid Fights about Money," *Huffington Post*, (March 13, 2012): https://www.huffingtonpost.com/2012/03/13/ financial-advice-couples-relationships_n_1340278.html.

13   Jesse Campbell, "Financial Stress Leads to Symptoms of Depression, PTSD," Money Management International, (May 2016): http://www.moneymanagement. org/Community/Blogs/Blogging-for-Change/2016/May/Financial-stress-leads-to-symptoms-of-depression.aspx.

the relationship that they may not fight for what's theirs. Sometimes, they're just too sad to stand up for themselves. When a death occurs, the survivors might be so sad that they lose control of their finances. They're simply too sad to care what happens to them.

CLIENT STORY
Coping and Counting

My client Susan sought my experience after losing her husband. Susan was in her late fifties, her kids were grown, and she resented having to be responsible for the finances after her husband died. She had never taken an interest in financial matters, having deferred to her husband on all financial decisions. When he died, Susan was left to make those decisions herself, so rather than manage her money, she started spending as she never had before. I felt her spending was almost a rebellion against having to take care of her own finances. She started improving her home, traveling, and buying things to fill the void left by her husband.

While this was happening, we talked to Susan about the impact her choices were having on her long-term plan to eventually retire. She could spend some of the money, but she couldn't continue doing it forever and expect to have any reasonable financial future. For a while, Susan's sadness kept her from focusing on the years still to come and understanding how her short-term spending was impacting her long-term choices. Finally, she realized that she was risking her financial future. This happened as we were talking about her three kids and how, if she kept spending at the rate she was spending, her choices would impact them. The idea that Susan's kids might have to be financially responsible for her in her later years was enough to help Susan turn her thinking around and take ownership of her finances. She accepted that, despite her sadness, she needed to start making decisions that were better aligned with her short- and long-term goals.

If left unchecked, fear, responsibility, excitement, and sadness can perpetuate financially disastrous behavior. Taking responsibility for the choices you make and looking at how your short-term choices can impact long-term outcomes can help you create a balance in your financial ecosystem.

How to Discover Your Own Money Story

Now that you see how emotions affect your money story and, as a result, impact your financial future, let's explore how to find your own money story.

When prospective clients visit Flourish, we give them two surveys that are designed to help them start to understand their own money story. The first is a financial satisfaction survey; the second is a life transitions survey—both of which can be accessed on my website at www.flourishwealthmanagement.com. The financial satisfaction survey is a twenty-point checklist that addresses everything from the client's spending habits to the level of debt carried, to investment choices. This helps give our clients perspective on how they currently feel about various aspects of their financial life.

The second survey looks at life transitions—marriage, death, retirement, etc.—which are key times when people look for guidance. Life transitions can be overwhelming, and can affect how people view and plan for their future. Knowing where you are regarding transitional periods will influence how you develop your future financial plans. We'll talk more about transitions in part 2 of this book. For now, let's examine something critical to discovering your money story: doing a values check.

DO A VALUES CHECK

To understand your own money story, you need to understand your values.

Have you ever known people who say they value their health, yet they never exercise and constantly eat fast food? So many of us say we value one thing and then engage in activities that don't support those values at all. In some situations, particularly when clients are struggling to articulate their money values, I will give them a one-page sheet of values—created by TurningPoint and located in this book's appendix—and ask them to choose their top twenty or thirty values and then gradually refine that list to between five and seven values. This process takes about five minutes and is very useful for helping people to specifically pinpoint their values.

Understanding values is so important to integrating the nine components that make up the Wheel of Life that at Flourish we require our staff to run through this exercise, too. It helps frame some of our conversations and our strategic planning processes at Flourish. It also helps us get on the same page about what's important to us as a team both professionally and personally.

For many clients, this conversation is the first time they clarify their values. This is because no one challenges us about money. No one engages us or gives us an opportunity to consciously think about what those values are. What does retirement actually mean? It's not just a dollars-and-cents equation. It's a lifestyle.

After we narrow our client's values down to five or seven different values, we ask clients substantive questions about each, such as, "What does this value mean to you? Tell me a little bit more about that."

This is how we get our clients to start digging into their money story. We ask questions like these because everyone defines family, financial independence, open-mindedness, and diversity differently. Financial independence, for example, means different things to different people. To me, it means owning my own business an spending my days doing what I love most. To others, it means having enough money to travel. Without really looking at your values, you can't honestly articulate your goals.

I wasn't truly in touch with my own values until I started conceptualizing Flourish. Until then, I didn't realize I needed to narrow in and focus on the things that are most important to me in order to achieve my goals. It took me a while, but I came up with the following core values:

- making a difference
- family
- financial independence
- philanthropy
- relationships
- open-mindedness
- wellness

Values can be tricky because sometimes they compete against each other. Before I started Flourish, I was hesitant to leave my firm because it provided financial security, which is a key value for me. However, after examining the rest of my values, I decided that I would let making a difference take precedence over financial independence in the hope that the trade-off would eventually bring me greater financial independence.

THE IMPORTANCE OF FINDING YOUR OWN VALUES

When I went through the process of finding my values, I realized how important it is to establish your own values around money and not be

I decided that I would let making a difference take precedence over financial independence in the hope that the trade-off would eventually bring me greater financial independence.

completely influenced by your family. Although your family's money values leave an imprint, you really need to sit down and think about how your values have evolved and changed over time.

Charitable Giving Insights

When talking about money values, charitable giving often comes up because, once you understand your own financial values and resources, you can start thinking about the joy that donating some of those resources might provide. Americans, as a whole, are generous with their money. According to Philanthropy Roundtable, two-thirds of Americans give money to a charitable organization annually.[14] If you're among those two-thirds, here are a few tips for getting the most give for your giving.

---

14   Philanthropy Roundtable, "Statistics," http://www.philanthropyroundtable.org/almanac/statistics/.

IDENTIFY THE CAUSES THAT ARE MOST IMPORTANT TO YOU.

Create a list of organizations that you've previously given to. Look at this list and consider which causes are most important to you so that, when you do give, your giving fully aligns with your values.

CONSIDER CONSOLIDATING YOUR GIFT.

Contrary to investing, diversification isn't always a good strategy when it comes to giving. Consolidating some of your giving may lead to greater impact. Focus on giving to a few key charities that most closely align with your core values. For example, if education is one of your key values, you may choose to focus on giving to educational organizations. In most cases, you will have more satisfaction and impact when you can focus on the nonprofits that mean the most to you instead of responding to every fund-raising request that comes in the mail.

INVOLVE THE FAMILY.

Giving can become part of your family tradition if you make an effort to involve the family in your giving process. First, have a family meeting that allows the kids to participate in your giving decisions. In addition to instilling the giving spirit early, this meeting provides an opportunity for family members to share individual perspectives about which causes are most important to them. Family members can develop their own traditions over time, including pooling money together, rotating the selection process for charities, and/or establishing a gift fund for kids to give from. Regardless of the dollar amount or organization selected, involving the family in the giving process will have long-term effects on your family and the charities they choose to give to.

LOOK BEYOND THE NUMBERS.

Giving doesn't always have to include a financial gift. It can be more about where you spend your time than where you spend your money. Donating your time may even make you feel more connected to an organization than if you gave the same organization money.

DO YOUR RESEARCH.

Once you know which charities match your giving goals, find the best ones to give to. Start by looking at the mission of the organization. It should align with your giving intentions. Next, look at the finances and general management of the organization, specifically what percentage of your donation will be absorbed by general management relative to how much will go toward the underlying cause. Online resources, including Charity Navigator, CharityWatch, Charities Review Council, and Guidestar are helpful.

MAXIMIZE YOUR GIFT.

Now that you (and potentially your family) have gone through the process of selecting where your charitable giving will go, it is important to follow a few important steps to maximize your gift. First, give directly. Many charities pay professional fundraisers from 40 to 80 percent of the proceeds received. Avoid donating to solicitors over the phone and give directly instead. In addition, try to avoid using credit cards to make your donation. Charities often pay 3 percent to 5 percent in credit card fees, immediately reducing the desired impact. Many employers also have matching programs that can be used whenever possible to increase the value of your gift. Finally, consider using appreciated assets as either a direct gift or through a donor-advised fund to incorporate additional tax savings.

DONOR-ADVISED FUNDS

Donor-advised funds are an important tool to consider including in your philanthropic efforts. These vehicles provide a flexible way to make a charitable contribution with cash or appreciated securities, take the full tax deduction at the time of the gift, and then easily make ongoing charitable contributions to the organizations of your choice. Donor-advised funds can be established at many large national organizations such as Charles Schwab, Fidelity, or Vanguard. In addition, there may be opportunities to create a donor-advised fund with a charitable organization in your community that aligns with your giving goals (I use Women's Foundation of Minnesota, for example, because my family supports their goal to create a world of equal opportunity for women and girls).

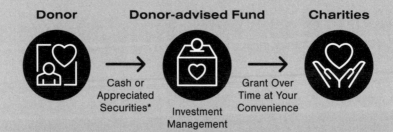

Donor **Donor-advised Fund** **Charities**

Cash or Appreciated Securities*

Investment Management

Grant Over Time at Your Convenience

Benefits:

capital gains tax avoidance and income tax deduction

Process:

- donate assets
- receive immediate tax benefits
- recommend investments
- make grants to charities
- plan for a charitable legacy

*Deduction for donated property is fair market value at time of donation. However, if appreciated securities are only held short-term, deduction is limited to cost basis.

Charitable giving is a process that should start at a level you feel comfortable with. Give when you feel secure about your own financial future—have a plan for your retirement, know what your future goals are, and understand that you have more than enough to give to charity.

Don't Focus on Numbers

You may have noticed that we're almost through the first chapter of *Flourish*. How many numbers have you seen? Very few. How many of them have been related to investment or savings goals? Zero. For a person who looks at numbers as part of her profession, I've written a book that is fairly devoid of numbers up to this point. There's a reason for that. I don't want you focusing on numbers and numbers alone. When we get *too* fixated on numbers, we get in our own way.

We let numbers drive our definition of success or happiness and lose sight of the experiences we want to create.

I discovered my own number fixation one day when I was shopping online. First, I fixated on the price of the shirts I was looking at. The price seemed too low, which made me question quality. The second number I fixated on was the size of the shirts. US sizes are larger than they are anywhere else in the world. A US eight or a US medium is much, much larger than it would be in Europe or South America, for example. The small sizes make consumers feel

> When we get too fixated on numbers, we get in our own way. We let numbers drive our definition of success or happiness and lose sight of the experiences we want to create.

better so they buy more. As I looked at the sizes of the clothes I was thinking about buying, I realized I was hesitating to buy these clothes because they didn't meet the "vanity sizing" standards. This discovery led to some analysis about how often our thoughts and opinions are dictated by specific numbers that, on their own, are often meaningless. We can become fixated on a specific number and, as a result, put everything else in our lives on hold—plans to work less, retire, buy a second home, or take a dream vacation—until we see that number on a spreadsheet. Instead of focusing on a quarterly report or a spreadsheet, we should focus on how we are progressing *overall* toward long-term planning goals. We should look at our values, what we want to do with our money, and what we want to do in our retirement and then figure out the numbers we need to have those experiences. Lifestyle and experience first, numbers second.

Life is far more meaningful when we stay focused on possibilities. Whether the goal is to change careers, retire early, or visit that foreign land you've always dreamed of, the focus should be on gaining clarity about what it takes to achieve your dreams. We should look at how we view money, our values, goals, and aspirations and then find the "real" number to make the life we pictured a reality.

Conversation Starters

1. What is your money story?

2. How was money and finance viewed and managed when you were growing up? What key experiences influence how you view money today?

3. How does fear, excitement, responsibility, and sadness affect how you spend, save, and invest money?

4. How satisfied are you with your current financial situation?

5. Are you going through any life transitions now that might affect how you manage your finances? If so, which ones?

6. What life transitions do you anticipate in the future?

7. What are your values?

8. How do your decisions support these values?

9. How are your values reflected in your charitable giving?

CHAPTER 2

Two Sides to Every Coin: Talking Finances with your Partner

Coming Together in Money Conversations

When I started Flourish, we knew we could live on Jay's salary from his business development position. It was great to have this financial backing. Jay estimated his new business commission for the next few years and we figured that even if Flourish didn't take off right away Jay would do well enough that we'd be financially set for a few years. So from my perspective of making financial security one of my top values, it seemed a good time to start my own business.

Unfortunately, Jay miscalculated his compensation in a big way. When we discovered the error, I thought, *Oh no! Now what do we do?* After apologizing and trying to explain the error in his calculations, Jay's response was, "It will all work out," which is always his response to money.

Jay encouraged me to pursue my dreams even though it felt risky financially and contradicted my belief in the value of financial security.

We launched Flourish, and then, about a year later, Jay lost his job. It created a bit of a wrench in our plan and required us to reexamine our financials as Flourish was still getting started and building toward long-term financial viability. Jay decided to look for a job that would allow him to get back into investment and retirement services, which is his passion. He ended up talking to some of our competitors, so we saw this as an opportunity to bring his expertise to the Flourish team. In the end, Jay's job situation worked out really well for us, but our conflicting views about money—I want security, Jay assumes everything will work out—created some tense moments.

Even if you are 100 percent in touch with your own values and money story, if you're sharing a life with someone you need to understand how that person views money as well. If you don't, compromising and achieving joint financial goals will be challenging. As we saw in chapter 1, money disagreements are a leading cause of divorce. Studies show that couples who fight about money once a week are 30 percent more likely to divorce than those who do not.[15]

HERE ARE SOME INFORMATIVE STATISTICS:[16]

- 31 percent of Americans who have combined their finances say they've lied to their spouse about money,
- 67 percent of these people said it caused arguments,
- 16 percent broke up as a result,
- 80 percent of couples spent secret money, and
- nearly 20 percent had a secret credit card.

---

15 Catherine Rampell, "Money Fights Predict Divorce Rates," *New York Times*, (December 7, 2009): https://economix.blogs.nytimes.com/2009/12/07/money-fights-predict-divorce-rates/#comment-90747.

16 Mark Bradshaw, "Love, Marriage and Financial Infidelity," http://ktul.com/archive/love-marriage-and-financial-infidelity.

Sonya Britt, researcher and assistant professor of family studies and human services and program director of financial planning at Kansas State University, conducted a study linking financial arguments to relationship satisfaction. She found that "arguments about money are by far the top predictor of divorce. It's not children, sex, in-laws, or anything else. It's money—for both men and women."[17]

Understanding your partner, how your partner views money, and how your partner values financial decisions may decrease the frequency and intensity of finance-based arguments.

Understand Your Partner's Money Story

Understanding your partner's financial story explains the motives behind your partner's approach to spending and saving. And when both partners understand where the other is coming from, it can help facilitate more compassion and compromise.

It's not uncommon for partners to have polar-opposite money stories. Take Jay and me as an example. We met at an investment class. Jay's background is in investment and retirement services for companies, while I have focused on individuals and families, so our professional backgrounds are a little different, but we are both in finance. Both Jay and I grew up in homes where frugality was valued. However, this value affected us differently.

Jay's mom grew up on a farm. The annual Christmas present from her parents was a butchered cow. Jay's family would take the cow home, fill up the freezer, and serve the cow for dinner for the rest

---

17   Money Habitudes, "Financial Statistics," https://www.moneyhabitudes.com/finan-cial-statistics/; Jacob Merkley, "Marriage and Finances: The Connection and Tips from 19 Marriage Experts," Power Over Life, (February 24, 2017): https://www.poweroverlife.com/marriage-finances-connection-tips/.

of the year. Jay is the only person I know who had to explain to his friends during junior high lunch what a tongue sandwich was.

Jay's dad was an attorney, but when Jay was a child, his dad was just getting established in his practice so the family didn't have a lot of money. To help pay the bills, Jay's mom worked outside the home and did what she could to reduce the family's spending. Jay's family made yogurt instead of buying it, and drank powdered milk because it was cheaper than fresh milk. To this day, Jay still won't drink milk. Our money stories are so powerful they can even create food aversions!

When Jay was ten, his first brother was born. When he was thirteen, his youngest brother arrived. Around this time, Jay noticed that his parents started spending more money. They started to invest in the house and buy nicer cars. This occurred for two reasons: (1) the family was growing, so there were more mouths to feed, and (2) Jay's dad was progressing in his career.

When Jay was twelve he started working as a caddy, but instead of saving his money he spent it on candy and hamburgers until it disappeared. That came to an end when Jay's dad asked him if he was saving his cash for the winter. That's when Jay started recording his earnings and saving them in a tin bucket.

Jay learned how to earn money and how to save it. He also learned how to manage it because his mom helped him open a checking account when he was quite young. But despite Jay's fairly conservative fiscal upbringing, his approach to money is much different from mine. Where I'm financially conservative, Jay's attitude toward money is relaxed: "It will all work out." As you can imagine, this dichotomy sometimes causes friction in our relationship.

TO START THE MONEY STORY CONVERSATION WITH YOUR SPOUSE OR PARTNER, ASK THE FOLLOWING QUESTIONS:

- What is your earliest memory of money?

- How did your family handle money when you were growing up?

- Whom would you describe as a role model in managing money?

- What are the best financial decisions that you have made?

- What decision about money do you regret?

- What early money messages did you receive that have stuck with you (e.g., "time is money")?

- How would you describe financial freedom?

Understand Your Partner's Values

We recommend that couples individually go through the values exercise mentioned in chapter 1 and share their personal outcome with each other. As I mentioned in chapter 1, my values are:

- making a difference
- family
- financial independence
- philanthropy
- relationships
- open-mindedness wellness

Jay's values are:

- authenticity—consistently representing his true self
- integrity/honesty—what he says is what he means
- family
- love
- fitness
- collaboration
- purpose

Jay and I share one core value: family. That certainly doesn't mean that Jay doesn't care about open-mindedness or that I don't care about integrity. It simply means that our seven core values are slightly different.

UNDERSTAND YOUR PARTNER

The way Jay and I felt about starting Flourish—a major life transition—was heavily influenced by our individual money stories and the emotions these stories evoked. While Jay's we'll-make-it-work attitude was difficult for me to understand at times, it also allowed him to enthusiastically support my idea to start my own business. While my desire to be financially secure sometimes might keep me from taking risks, it also keeps me from taking risks that are too great.

While my huge focus on financial independence is one of my core values, Jay does not make money or financial independence part of his core values. Jay defers to me for all financial decisions. We both have access to Mint, an app and online platform that helps people easily track their spending (which I set up), but Jay doesn't look at it. This can make me feel resentful or financially lonely because, ultimately, it's up to me to make the finances work. However, when you understand your partner's values and money story, you can better understand your partner's attitude toward money. I understand that

Jay cares about our finances, but I also understand his approach to managing them is different from mine.

Understanding your partner's money story and values will help clarify how and why your partner makes financial decisions. This can help bring you both to a common ground, which is necessary when you start looking at your joint financial future.

For a list of values to review with your partner, go to the appendix.

Be Honest about the State of Your Current Finances

When Jay and I first started dating I was in a transition period. As I already mentioned, transition periods—divorces, marriages, career changes, and death—can have a huge impact on your finances, your values, and your money story. The transition I was going through was a job change, so I was very focused on work. Six months into the relationship, Jay and I were engaged and decided to move in together. This meant that both of us not only had to sell houses but also choose a new house to buy, so the conversations we had planned to have about our joint financial future were pushed off longer than we would have liked.

We talked about how much we could sell our houses for, and we also had the basic money talk: "These are my assets; what are your assets?" But we didn't have an in-depth financial conversation until later in our relationship. Ideally, you want to have basic financial conversations with your partner as part of the decision to get married. Specifically, you want to talk about assets and liabilities, income and expenses, and your general approach to financial management.

ASSETS AND LIABILITIES

You should know all of your individual and combined assets and liabilities and where they fall on the family balance sheet.

INCOME AND EXPENSES

Know how much you and your partner are making and saving and why you're choosing to save that amount. If you're not saving enough, see where you can start driving down expenses.

KNOW YOUR CREDIT SCORE

In addition to the money values and assets a person brings into a relationship, their credit score is an important aspect of their money history. I've seen couples that have significant assets, good income, and a healthy ability to save end up with poor credit scores because they don't keep up with monthly payments or because one person brought a lot of debt into the relationship. As a result, their credit scores take a hit, which is unfortunate because low credit scores can impact your ability to achieve your financial goals. Even if you are not managing the household finances, know your and your partner's credit score. These scores can unveil existing financial issues that may need to be cleared up before you move forward with your financial future. Many financial institutions or credit card providers offer this number for free.

Facing Reality

I worked with one couple who experienced a nasty surprise when we pulled both of their credit reports. The woman had deferred all financial decisions to her husband so she was shocked when she read his credit report, which revealed a sizeable debt. The husband accrued the debt because he was more focused on living in the moment than he was on the future. However, because his debts would affect their future plans, the couple made a decision to clear his debt and start saving. He even felt relief by coming clean on this debt and having a plan to move forward.

There are a lot of important money conversations that need to take place before a couple gets married, and these same topics will continue to be important after the wedding. A big part of my role as a financial planner is to help my client couples walk through these critical financial conversations. In addition, I also have them sit down and go through some key financial documents including:

KEY FINANCIAL DOCUMENTS TO GATHER AND DISCUSS WITH YOUR SPOUSE

- life insurance policies

- disability policies

- auto, homeowners, and umbrella policies

- long-term care policies

- information on medical policies

- business owners—buy-sell agreements, key person insurance policies

- most recent federal and state tax returns including all schedules

- bank and investment statements including details of investment holdings for all personal and retirement accounts

- paystubs

- Social Security estimate of benefits

- employee benefit information including stock options or employee stock purchase plans

- statements for mortgages, lines of credit, or other debt

- current credit score

- cash flow and spending information

- wills, trusts, health care directives and powers of attorney

Jointly looking through these documents puts you on the same page regarding the state of your current saving, spending, protecting, and investing.

I can't tell you how many times a Flourish couple will go through this exercise and one of the spouses will say, "I didn't know there was this *X, Y, Z* banking account." Oftentimes, the spouse with the "secret" account will insist on retaining that private account. Some people really need financial resources that are not linked to their partner because it gives them a greater sense of independence. The point is, even if an account remains private to one individual, both spouses should know about it.

Define Your Roles

Every couple has their own system for managing money. The key is to develop that system early so you know who manages the finances and how they're managed. In addition to talking to your spouse about your current financial status, have conversations about money management. For example, how will credit card debt be handled? Some spouses are okay with having some amount of debt, while others say absolutely not. How will you manage large purchases? Do you talk to each other about every purchase that is over $200, $500, or $1,000? Do you put your money into one shared account, or do you each have your own account with a joint account for shared household expenses? Who pays the day-to-day bills? Who manages the investments? Talk to your spouse about these decisions and then agree to sit down quarterly and review your finances together.

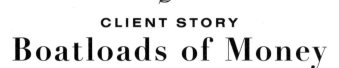

CLIENT STORY
Boatloads of Money

I worked with one client, Sharon, who never looked at her finances, which were managed by her husband. Sharon would say, "Oh, he's in charge of the finances. I'm not really interested." Unfortunately, Sharon's husband ended up spending their money recklessly, which put her in a financial bind. He bought boats and other large-ticket items, and when she asked about those purchases he reassured her that everything was fine. Eventually, payments were missed, and when they ultimately divorced Sharon learned that her husband had spent all of the proceeds from the business he had sold on unnecessary items.

Even after you have the conversations mentioned in this chapter, you will still have financial disagreements with your spouse because even couples with the most effective money management systems still argue over money. It seems we just can't help but argue over finance.

You Spent What on What?

While you and your spouse may disagree about certain spending patterns, understanding how your partner views money, where you, as a couple, stand financially, and how your finances will be managed can minimize these disagreements.

TOP FIVE MONEY ARGUMENTS[18]

46%	**33%**	**26%**	**25%**	**22%**
Frivolous Purchases	Household Budgeting	Credit Card Debt	Insufficient Emergency Savings	Insufficient Retirement Funds

Sometimes a package or two will arrive on the porch that Jay doesn't know about. Other times, we'll forget to communicate or miscommunicate over expenses. Once, Jay had to get his car repaired, and while he was doing that he discovered he needed new tires. Because our money roles have me managing the money, when an unexpected $1,200 bill came through I was annoyed. I said, "What is this bill?" He said, "The tires needed to be replaced." He said it casually because, to Jay, it was something that needed to be done so he got it done without discussion. It wasn't a huge argument, but it brought us to an important agreement that's helped to prevent other money disagreements: we agreed that we'd talk about any unexpected expenses that exceeded $500.

Financial advisors help couples find a middle ground by:
- facilitating tough financial conversations,
- creating a common language that the couple can use at home and in meetings,
- building a foundation for future money conversations,
- engaging both spouses in all conversations, and
- identifying goals and objectives for the individual and the couple.

---

18 Cybele Weisser, and Kerri Anne Renzulli, "Seven Ways to Stop Fighting about Money and Grow Richer, Together," *Time*: Money, June 1, 2014, http://time.com/money/2791658/couples-marriage-money-survey-female-breadwinners/.

THE THERAPIST'S COUCH

Even though Jay and I have been married for fifteen years, when we talk about money, it's often like sitting on the therapist's couch. For example, when Jay joined Flourish and both of us were focused on the business, we had to have a hard conversation about one of us focusing more on our career and the other focusing more on the family.

We reprioritized how we would look at things. My role at Flourish is growing and thriving and needs a lot of attention, so we decided that Jay would take on more of the household responsibilities and be the main lead with the kids for now. Although we compromised, it was a hard decision for both of us. I was slightly resentful of the change. I have traditional values and like the idea of the mother taking the lead on the kids and the home. However, Jay and I view our marriage as a unit and knew this decision was the right one for our family. I would add that Jay has become quite the chef in our house.

No matter how open the lines of communication are with your partner, talking about money is often like sitting on a therapist's couch. It delves into your childhood, plays on your emotions, and requires facing difficult conversations head-on.

Agree on a Financial Future

Conversations about money aren't easy, but you need to have them in order to achieve your goals. Once you outline the good, the bad, and the ugly of your own finances, you can sit down with your partner and agree on a financial future. While finance is the premise for talking about a financial future, this conversation isn't just about dollars and cents. It's a much deeper conversation about how you're going to achieve the shared vision you have for your lives.

Some people want to retire and travel. Others want to take a mid-career break and join the Peace Corps for a few years. Planning a financial future together means taking what you know of your past, your present, and what you desire of your future and setting a foundation for a life vision. Once you do that, you can take actionable steps to achieve that vision.

Tips for Planning Your Future

CHOOSE THE RIGHT ENVIRONMENT

Before you sit down with your partner to discuss your financial future, pick the right space and timing. If Jay and I had talked about our collective financial future after a long, trying workday, we wouldn't have gotten very far. Or if we had discussed it in an environment that makes one of us tense, it wouldn't have set the correct tone for the meeting.

TALK TO THE RIGHT ADVISOR

Many couples come to me because they feel their current advisor is only meeting the needs of one of them. Maybe the advisor only talks to one of the spouses. Maybe the advisor uses too much industry jargon when meeting with the couple. Whatever the reason, if you decide to work with a financial advisor, make sure that professional is meeting your needs and your spouse's. Your relationship with your advisor will affect your financial goals, so make sure you're with someone who is right for you.

Conversation Starters

1. What is your spouse's money story and how does it affect his/her spending and saving decisions?

2. As a couple, how will you manage your finances?

3. Do you both get a checking account and a separate credit card, and/or will there be some sort of joint account?

4. Is there a spending limit where one spouse must consult the other before making a purchase?

5. What values do you share?

6. What values conflict and how might this affect your future financial plans?

7. What is your shared vision for the future and what steps do you need to take to achieve that vision?

8. What are your fears around money?

CHAPTER 3

Women, Wealth, and Wisdom

I was at an industry conference a few years ago listening to Sallie Krawcheck when the challenges that women face in building their wealth became painfully obvious to me. Sallie Krawcheck is one of the most successful women in the wealth management industry, having held prominent leadership positions with large Wall Street firms. Sallie Krawcheck often speaks about giving women the resources and encouragement to manage their finances, along with many other important themes that address pay inequality and lack of diversity in corporate leadership. She is an incredibly successful, intelligent woman, and I felt grateful for having the opportunity to not only listen to her speak but to also sit at her lunch table.

During her keynote speech, which was about women and their planning needs, she asked the audience, comprised of financial professionals, "What's a woman's greatest asset?" Immediately, several members of the audience murmured, "A man."

Sallie was actually asking about a woman's ability to create earning power and save for the future, and about the opportunities she has to maximize the possibility of building a successful long-term plan with an effective wealth management relationship, yet the audience immediately deferred to "a man" as a woman's greatest asset. I thought, *Oh my gosh! This is really sad.* As sad as it is, this response speaks to two large issues within financial services: (1) many women don't feel heard or part of the financial conversation, and (2) the majority of financial planners don't engage in the bigger picture purpose for the dollars.

A Man is Not a Plan

A good 80 percent of Sallie Krawcheck's audience was male, which is representative of my industry. Only 23 percent of certified financial planners are women, and of the 311,000 financial advisers in the US, only 15.7 percent are women, a statistic that has been stubbornly consistent over many decades, and the financial advice industry as a whole doesn't know how to speak to women or learn what they want.[19]

In some circles, there is a lingering feeling that women take a backseat when it comes to finance and, instead, let their spouses manage their accounts. This couldn't be further from the truth. Women's wealth and their ability to make money are growing faster than ever. Currently, women control $14 trillion of personal wealth, or 51 percent of wealth; in the next five years, this is expected to increase to $18 trillion.[20] Now, more than ever, women have larger incomes and a greater desire to take control of their financial futures.

Even though women are taking control of their finances, their experiences with the investment world are lacking. According to a study conducted by global research firm EY, women say their experi-

---

19 Jeff Benjamin, "How to Improve Gender Diversity in Financial Advice," Investment News, (March 12, 2018): http://www.investmentnews.com/article/20180312/ FREE/180319993/how-to-improve-gender-diversity-in-financial-advice?itx[idio]=620 4338&ito=792&itq=2621fc7b-6eb2-419a-bad7-de04a9755802.

20 *Women and Wealth: The Case for a Customized Approach*, report, EY, 2017.

ences with the investment world are "unwelcoming," "patronizing," "male dominated," and "full of jargon."[21]

Sixty-seven percent of female investors perceive that their banker or wealth manager "misunderstands their goals or cannot empathize with their lifestyle."[22] Unfortunately, I see this all the time. Women tell me that, in the past, when meeting with a financial planner they either didn't have a comfortable conversation about their finances or goals, were presented with options that were too laden with jargon for them to ask important follow-up questions, or they were made to feel they didn't have a voice.

While some women are comfortable with relying on their husbands to make financial decisions, as Sallie Krawcheck said when she responded to the murmurs about men being a woman's best asset, a man is not a plan. In fact, the majority of women will be responsible for their own finances at some point in their life whether they like it or not. This might happen when they first leave school, when they go through a divorce, or when they continue into retirement after their spouse dies.

DON'T THINK YOU'LL BE ALONE? THINK AGAIN

- Regardless of whether they were married earlier in life, many women will be single at some point during their retirement years. Over half (54 percent) of women age sixty-five and older were single in 2014, according to US Census Bureau data.[23]

---

21 Ibid.
22 Ibid.
23 Marylene LaPonsie, "Many Women Will Be Single in Retirement. Are You Ready?" US News & World Report, (September 23, 2016): https://money.usnews.com/money/personal-finance/articles/2016-09-23/many-women-will-be-single-in-retirement-are-you-ready

- A woman turning sixty-five today can expect to live until an average age of eighty-seven.[24]

- When it comes to retirement readiness, a study by the education firm Financial Finesse found that a forty-five-year-old woman needs to save an additional $522,000 by age sixty-five to cover her expenses.[25]

Build Confidence

One-third of women find talking about money stressful compared to just under a quarter of men.[26] Even worse, women don't always want to talk about money or seek help when they have questions about managing it. In my experience, this is due in large part to lack of confidence.

Whether you are male or female, to increase your confidence in making financial decisions follow these ten easy steps.

STEP 1: UNDERSTAND YOUR SPENDING

Forty-one percent of Americans spend *less* money than they make, so the majority of us are spending about what we make or *more* than we make.[27] Understanding your spending habits is the first step toward building financial confidence.

---

24   Emily Brandon, "How to Estimate Your Life Expectancy," US News & World Report, (March 21, 2016): https://money.usnews.com/money/retirement/articles/2016-03-21/how-to-estimate-your-life-expectancy.

25   Eleanor Laise, "Savvy Retirement Moves for Women," *Kiplinger's Retirement Report*, (July 2016): https://www.kiplinger.com/article/retirement/T047-C000-S004-savvy-retirement-moves-for-women.html.

26   "Women Backwards in Coming Forward When it Comes to Money Matters," Money Advice Service, press release, November 21, 2011: https://www.moneyadviceservice.org.uk/files/20111121_pressrelease.pdf.

27   "Seven Things Every Woman Should Do To Get Her Finances in Order," Mussett Wealth Management, http://www.mussettwealth.com/7-things-every-woman-should-do-to-get-her-finances-in-order/.

All spending can be divided into two categories: (1) critical spending, and (2) nice-to-have spending. Critical or necessary spending includes everything you need to live. This group of expenses includes your rent or mortgage payment, health insurance, copays, and utility bills to name a few. These fixed expenses are critical to your day-to-day existence. Nice-to-haves, on the other hand, aren't necessary for day-to-day living. They are just that: nice to have. These expenses might include this season's jacket, a vacation, or a phone upgrade.

Understanding the difference between these two kinds of expenses will help you budget and know which expenses to cut back on when needed.

NECESSARY VS. NICE-TO-HAVE

- Utility bills	- Vacations
- Mortgage payment	- Latest fashion trends
- Health insurance	- Phone upgrades

STEP 2: UNDERSTAND YOUR DEBT

Debt can be a little tricky because there's good debt and bad debt. As a general rule, good debt facilitates a goal. Buying a house or taking out student loans can lead to good debt. The house might be a long-term investment and the student loan debt might help you pursue that career you know you'll thrive in. Of course, you don't want to get in a situation where you can't pay off the student loan or the house debt.

FACTS ABOUT STUDENT LOAN DEBT[28]

- US student loan debt accounts for $1.48 trillion.

- There are 44.2 million Americans with student loan debt.

- The average monthly student loan payment (for borrowers aged twenty to thirty years) is $351.

Bad debt, on the other hand, is debt that includes a high interest rate and doesn't necessarily support a life goal. The most common bad debt in the US is credit card debt. The average American has $15,654 in credit card debt.[29] The thing is, many people don't see credit card debt as bad debt. They have no idea that they're paying 18 percent interest (or more) on debts of $5,000 or $15,000. And if they pay the minimum payments, their payment goes right toward the interest and doesn't make a dent in how much they owe. The amount they're paying interest on increases as they add new charges, but many people think small purchases don't matter because they don't fully understand the importance of reducing debt.

STEP 3: BUILD AN EMERGENCY FUND

Life brings many ups, downs, and surprises. These are inevitable. What you can control is how you handle financial surprises as they come along. What if family members become sick and you have to take a leave of absence from work or absorb the costs associated with caring for them? What happens if you or your spouse lose a job?

Job loss can have a drastic effect on your finances. If the labor

---

28 "A Look at the Shocking Student Loan Debt Statistics for 2018," Student Loan Hero, updated January 24, 2018: https://studentloanhero.com/student-loan-debt-statistics/.

29 Erin El Issa, "NerdWallet's 2017 American Household Credit Card Debt Study," NerdWallet.com, https://www.nerdwallet.com/blog/average-credit-card-debt-household/.

market is tight, or if you have a very specialized skill, or if you get paid very well, finding a new job can take months. Having an emergency fund can help you through the transition period after a job loss.

I recommend having three to six months of living expenses stored away as your emergency fund. This will go a long way toward paying for any unexpected expenses such as a car repair bill, an unexpected medical bill, or costs of living during a job loss when life hands you one of its many surprises.

Sometimes, couples choose to live off of one earner's income and save the rest. For a single person, acquiring three to six months of income reserve can be challenging. Start working toward saving one or two paychecks for an emergency fund and go from there.

STEP 4: SAVE EARLY

When you save early, setting up an emergency fund is far less daunting.

When you first have income—or when you start your first "real job"—start saving 10 to 15 percent of your income. Not only is this good for your emergency fund, but it gets you in the habit of saving. It makes your future part of your present, day-to-day activities when you decide to "pay yourself first" with a healthy savings habit.

STEP 5/CLIENT STORY
Learn the Lingo

I recently sat in on a meeting with a client, Jennifer, and an advisor from another firm whom my client was required to work with, as this firm managed a trust for her son's benefit. The advisor was giving an update on a trust account that was set up for the benefit of Jennifer's son. It was evident to everyone in the room that the company could have been managing the account more effectively. During the update, the advisor frequently dipped into financial jargon, such as, "Our Monte Carlo analysis says ... "

Before I knew it, I found myself playing translator for Jennifer. Similar to most people, she didn't know anything about Monte Carlo analyses, or why this was part of her investment strategy. Most people don't know this term, but the advisor continued talking about Monte Carlo analysis and using other financial jargon such as duration, yield, and P/E ratios while talking to Jennifer. She was totally lost, and I wondered if the advisor was using jargon to make himself sound good, or confuse the client, or because he just wasn't aware of the effect his terms were having.

At one point, Jennifer asked why the fund was so conserva-tive. When the advisor said he didn't want to take too much risk while the market recovered. Jennifer said, "Well didn't the market crash in 2008?" He said yes. She said, "Well, wouldn't there have been a good time to have more equity and stock exposure at some point in the past nine years?" He said, "Well, in hindsight, yes."

It turns out Jennifer knew what she was talking about. The advisor would often use jargon throughout his presenta-tion, deterring her from asking additional valid follow-up questions.

My advice to all women is this: do not let jargon scare you away from taking charge of your finances. Yes, the terms are confusing, but with time and patience the terminology becomes approachable. Learning how to speak finance is like learning a new language. Be patient with it, speak up when you don't understand, and take a look at the list of commonly misunderstood terms that I've created to help improve your confidence when you speak with your advisor.

FINANCIAL JARGON DEFINED

- *Asset allocation*: the percentage of your portfolio invested in stocks, bonds, and other investments
- *Diversification*: strategy of mixing different types of investments to reduce overall risk (a.k.a., not having all your eggs in one basket)
- *Expense ratio*: how much you are paying the company that manages your investments
- *Mutual funds:* combine money from many people to invest in stocks, bonds, or other assets to create a portfolio. Each investor in the fund owns shares which represent their portion of the mutual fund.
- *Index funds*: type of mutual fund that tracks a broad market, like the S&P 500 Index
- *Monte Carlo analysis:* modeling technique of running simulations over and over to see if you can reach your goals.
- *Market risk*: the chance you could lose money because your investments will move up or down without your control. Examples include stocks, bonds, real estate, or other investments.

- *RMD (required minimum distribution)*: the minimum dollar amount IRA owners must withdraw each year, beginning when they reach age seventy-and-a-half, as required by the IRS
- *Standard deviation:* range of expected investment outcomes to provide perspective on riskiness of an investment; higher standard deviation generally means more risk.

STEP SIX: AVOID LIFESTYLE CREEP

"Lifestyle creep" occurs when we increase our spending as our income increases rather than choosing to save some of that additional income, and occurs for three reasons: (1) people don't have a plan for what they want to do with additional income, (2) people live too much for today, so they think of ways to spend "extra" money rather than planning for the future, or (3) people spend far too much time comparing themselves to others. I can't tell you how many people come to me and say, "Well shouldn't we be able to do that? So-and-so said that they're able to take this trip (or buy this fancy car) and they make less than we do."

The comparison trap is dangerous. There are unknown circumstances going on behind the scenes financially for every family. It's impossible to tell whether your neighbors can actually afford whatever it is they're buying. Perhaps they are thousands of dollars in debt. Maybe they're about to start foreclosure proceedings. Maybe they inherited a large sum of money. The point is you never know what others can truly afford or why they can afford it.

Be Leery of Outside Opinions

I advise a young newlywed couple, Todd and Heather, who make a good living while being financially independent and financially responsible. For a long time Heather's parents encouraged them to buy a house. The parents compared renting to wasting money. To them, it made more sense to invest in a house than "throw money away" on rent. Todd and Heather disagreed. They loved living in their trendy neighborhood and with lots of interesting restaurants, social activities, and friends nearby. It was a part of the city where they could not afford to buy a home but could afford the high rent. They felt that this would be their only opportunity to live in this neighborhood and fully enjoy the social lifestyle, so they made the decision to delay buying a house until the time was right for them. This was a good decision for my clients, as they enjoyed their lives in the trendy neighborhood until eventually moving out and buying a house when they decided to grow their family. Sometimes it's important to consider personal experiences and lifestyle, even if they aren't always considered the "best" financial decision.

Be cautious when heeding advice from nonprofessionals. Like Heather's parents, most people don't give financial advice to harm you. They usually intend to help. However, if they don't know your situation or what's right for you, their advice can do more harm than good. We also tend to cherry-pick the details of our financial stories.

So if you hear that some other people got a loan from their portfolio so they could buy their house and it turned out to be a great decision, that might only be half of the story. Perhaps these people also made a large down payment with money from an inheritance. Maybe in the end they didn't get any value out of the house, so they lost money. We tend to hear the rosy side of other people's financial pictures. Make sure you're not getting a revamped version of what really happened.

If you accept financial advice from others, make sure you're close to them and that you respect their financial decisions.

STEP 8: KNOW YOUR NUMBER

Your credit score paints a picture of your current financial status. Everyone should know their credit score. Your credit score examines your amount owed, new credit, length of credit history, credit mix, and payment history.

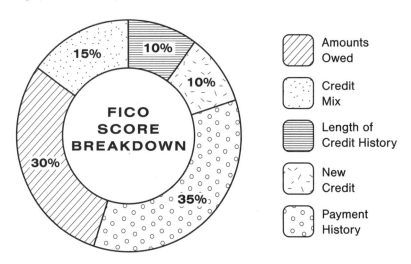

Credit card companies will often post a snapshot of your credit score to your online account. Apps such as Mint are also a great way to track your credit score and your spending.

STEP 9: NEGOTIATE YOUR SALARY

Even though women control more than half of the country's wealth and are expected to control even more within the next five years, the income discrepancy between male and female earners remains an issue, as women continue to earn seventy-seven cents for every dollar earned by men. The statistics are even more alarming for women of color.[30]

Gaining the confidence to ask for a raise when it's well deserved or negotiating a salary based on your skill level rather than your gender will not only boost your income but also raise your overall fiscal confidence. This isn't always easy to do, even for the most accomplished women.

One of my clients is a doctor. In addition to her day-to-day duties, she ended up taking on some management responsibilities. However, her compensation was never adjusted to account for the extra work she was doing. With our support, she went back and asked for a higher salary based on the additional work she was doing, and was able to get the compensation she deserved.

STEP 10: HIRE A FINANCIAL PLANNER EARLY

One of my clients hired a financial planner when she was thirty. She ranks that among one of the top-five best decisions she's ever made.

Hiring a financial planner well before retirement gave this client a lifelong financial partner. It also gave her a solid financial foundation that allowed her to save early, examine her expenses, and know what she personally wanted from her finances before she married. It's also given her a go-to person for any financial questions she has.

If you hire a financial advisor early in your career, make sure you're comfortable talking to that person about your financial goals. Seventy percent of women leave their financial advisor after a major

---

30 "Gap Analysis: What Equal Pay Day Gets Wrong," PayScale, https://www.payscale.com/data-packages/gender-pay-gap.

life change such as the death of a spouse or divorce, suggesting that most women are not happy with their current advisor.[31]

> ## BY THE NUMBERS: WHY WOMEN SHOULD FEEL INVESTMENT CONFIDENT[32]
>
> - Women make an average of 0.4 percent more on their investments than men, which can be a significant advantage over time.
> - Women save 0.4 percent more of their paychecks than men. They also add 0.8 percent more to savings accounts outside workplace savings.
> - Women are more patient investors than men.
> - Women are more likely to consider life goals when developing their financial plans than men.

Let Go of Your Fears

Building confidence also allows us to let go of some of the fears that hold us back from making financial decisions, fears that can prevent us from achieving our life dreams. If I allowed my fears about owning my own firm to take hold, I wouldn't have the opportunity to truly follow my passions as an entrepreneur-planner.

Following is a list of the fourteen most common fears expressed by women as they look to take charge of their finances.

---

31   Judy Paradi and Paulette Filion, "Why Women Leave Their Financial Advisors," Strategy Marketing, http://www.academia.edu/12142219/ Why_Women_Leave_Their_Financial_Advisors.

32   "Who's the Better Investor: Men or Women?" Fidelity Investments, press release, May 18, 2017: https://www.fidelity.com/about-fidelity/individual-investing/ better-investor-men-or-women.

1. losing a job

2. not having enough money to pay bills or retire

3. "bag lady" syndrome, or fear of living on the streets

4. fear of numbers (numerophobia), or lack of confidence in working with or understanding numbers

5. saying no to kids, disappointing kids, and worrying that the kids won't succeed

6. messing up kids by giving them too much, creating too much dependence

7. investments that lose money

8. taking too much risk

9. being a burden on family because, later in life, they may need care

10. losing a sense of identity—this particularly applies to career women at retirement

11. losing inherited dollars or failing to carry on the legacy

12. fear of failure

13. fear of missing out and taking on too much risk

14. fear of retirement and its impact on marriage

The fear of numbers, or numerophobia, is the fear I hear most often, particularly from married women who are accustomed to letting their husbands take the lead on household finances. It's a first line of defense for women who are resistant to or uninterested in having financial conversations. I try to remind my clients that most people know how to add and subtract. With a little bit more information, these basic skills are really all you need to manage your money.

Several years ago, a male prospect who eventually became a client contacted me to set our first meeting. Shortly after our call, he sent an email confessing that he hadn't looked at his financial statements for three years. He added that he didn't know much about finance. This is the first and only time I've had a male client express this fear.

I also consistently hear women express the fear that they don't want to be a burden. Their fear is that their kids will have to take care of them during retirement. Really, it's a fear of running out of money, but for women, this fear tends to manifest as not wanting to negatively affect their family.

In my experience, the majority of fears women have about finance derive from avoidance. Quite simply, they delay dealing with their finances until a transition such as divorce, inheritance, or being recently widowed forces them to get involved. But getting involved with finances shouldn't be a reactive situation. I recommend confronting these fears and taking a proactive financial role in the following ways:

- building your confidence in making financial decisions,

- developing a financial plan,

- ignoring sensational messages from the media that can confirm some of your gravest fears,

- considering the longer timeframe and how it affects the management of your funds, and

- having the conversations we are having in this book.

Take an Interest

One difference I've noticed between male and female investors is that female investors are much more interested than male investors are in how their goals affect other areas of their life. If I can show a female investor how goal X will pay for her kids' college, allow her and her husband to continue traveling, and ensure that she doesn't become a burden to her children during retirement, she'll be far more inclined to show an interest in her financial future.

When I first met my clients Tonya and Marc, it was clear that Tonya deferred her investment and financial decisions to Marc. When we invited them to the initial meeting, Marc said of Tonya, "You might see her at this meeting, but it will be the only one. She's not that interested in numbers."

During that first meeting, we not only talked about financial goals but also about the best way to fund their kids' education. Once we started talking about the purpose of the money, Tonya became extremely engaged. Marc still manages the day-to-day finances, but she's still engaged and comes to every meeting.

If you're struggling to become interested in finance, stop making it about the numbers and, instead, focus on the goals and possibilities your investments can bring. Instead of thinking about bottom-line dollars and cents, ask yourself the following:

- If money were no object, how would I spend my time?

- What would I do more of? What would I do less of?

- What would I need to do financially to achieve these goals?

Tips for Getting Excited about Your Finances

- Break your cash flow into bite-size pieces and focus on these three components:
  1. mastering the day-to-day bill paying, living within your means, and understanding your income;
  2. understanding both short and long-term goals; and
  3. saving and investing to match those goals.

- Psychology is more important than dollars and cents. Return to your money story and understand where your feelings about money come from.

- Substitute industry jargon for comfortable conversation.

- Identify steps that can be taken on a daily, weekly, and monthly basis to achieve your goals.

- Schedule time to review your investments and financial plan.

- Create a connection with a financial advisor.

- Turn to online and workplace education.

- Talk to trusted friends.

- Connect to other professional providers who can help, such as an accountant, estate attorney, and personal insurance agent.

Finance doesn't have to be thought of as all budget and restriction. With some reframing, this can be an exciting conversation. Finances are a tool that allows us to take control of our lives and achieve our life goals and dreams.

Conversation Starters

1. What prevents you from talking about and becoming actively involved in your financial management?

2. What can you do today to boost your confidence in managing your finances?

3. What lifestyle outcomes—paying for your children's college, starting a business, traveling, donating to charities—will motivate you to pay closer attention to your financial numbers?

4. Which of the fourteen fears apply to you?

5. What can you do to overcome those fears?

PART 2
Transitions

Disasters often strike with little notice. Some such as the major hurricanes of 2017—Hurricanes Harvey, Irma, Jose, and Maria—are the product of Mother Nature. Others, such as the Equifax security breach of 2017, are man-made. While natural and man-made disasters may seem to have little in common, they all leave financial devastation in their wake.

Hurricane Harvey alone destroyed 12,700 homes and damaged more than 203,000 others.[33] The Equifax breach affected the personal data of more than 4.6 million people, forcing nearly five million Americans to worry about their financial security and potential exposure to identity theft.[34]

The financial damage inflicted by these man-made and natural disasters was enormous. While homes can be repaired, the dire concerns victims of disasters have about their financial futures produces untold anxiety that adds to the stress of the disaster. A change in a person's career, family, or lifestyle (retirement), can have the same effect.

I meet and help many people when they are in the midst of experiencing big changes in their career, family, or lifestyle. We refer to these changes as life transitions. Whether your transition is due to the sale of a business, the loss of a spouse, the receipt of an inheritance, or a combination of several transitions, it is often difficult. Successfully moving through a major life transition is a balancing act of owning the moment while also planning for the future and finding a way to embrace your next steps.

---

33   Kimberly Amadeo, "Hurricane Harvey Facts, Damage and Costs," The Balance, (February 13, 2018): https://www.thebalance.com/hurricane-harvey-facts-damage-costs-4150087.

34   "Michigan AG: Ways to Protect ID after Equifax Data Breach," CBS Detroit, (October 9, 2017): http://detroit.cbslocal.com/2017/10/09/michigan-ag-ways-to-protect-id-after-equifax-data-breach/.

It is said that change is the only constant in life, yet the lack of certainty that change brings is often overwhelming. While change is constant, transition is temporary. There is light at the end of the tunnel, but getting to that light requires planning. Throughout part 2, we will look at each of life's major transitions and discuss how we can best prepare for each so that, when they inevitably occur, we can find a way to the light.

CHAPTER 4

Nickels and Dimes: When Change Happens

J ust as we were celebrating Flourish's one-year anniversary, Jay called while I was at work and said, "I'm losing my job."

I couldn't believe it. As I've mentioned before, our plan was to live off Jay's good, steady income while I grew the business. My plan was to not take an income from the business in the early stages because we thought that after two to three years of investing all of the profits back into our team and resources, Flourish would have the staffing structure that would allow us to provide the high level of service we'd always dreamed of. With a single phone call, that plan was flipped on its head. I didn't know how Jay and I would support our family, or how we'd have the resources to grow Flourish.

In addition to worrying about the financial implications of Jay's unexpected career transition, Jay and I had to cope with some overwhelming emotions. Unexpected career changes such as losing a job often trigger feelings of shame in those who have lost their job. At the time, Jay viewed his role in the family and the marriage, in part, as a financial contributor. When Jay talked to people about his job loss, he explained the change as an agreement between himself and his employer. Not only was he ashamed about losing his job, he was afraid of the unknown. He was afraid that he wouldn't find another job, afraid that his job loss would affect Flourish, and afraid that his firing would negatively impact our family. While Jay experienced feelings of fear and shame, I experienced anger. I wanted to know why Jay couldn't make his job situation work, even though I knew he had been unhappy in his position at the company.

Following his job loss, Jay and I worried about how our family would afford certain expenses. We hoped and prayed that Flourish would thrive to offset that lost compensation. When any transition affects your finances, it's often difficult to come to an acceptance of the situation and move forward. Once we stopped hoping, we started working. First we reacted, and then we acted.

We went back to our financial plan, redid our numbers, cut back on certain budget items, and continued working through our strategy to make Flourish grow, which, fortunately, it has. We also took a new approach to Jay's job search. When we removed our reactionary emotions from the situation, we realized that Jay was actually applying for jobs with companies that competed with Flourish. That didn't make sense. So Flourish hired Jay, which was a great decision.

Career Transitions

Career transitions are sometimes unexpected, but if we know *how* they might occur, they're easier to plan for. Career changes usually happen because someone decides to change their career path, has a job loss, scales back working hours, or experiences a disability. We'll talk about a fifth career change—retirement—in chapter six.

CHANGES IN CAREER PATH

Changes in a career path may include going back to school, working beyond your anticipated retirement age, a job promotion, a layoff, a recession, or a change in income (an increase or decrease).

Karen was in her early thirties when she walked into our office. She was very successful. An engineer at a large firm, she used her skills to oversee plant operations for one of her company's clients. Karen was doing well financially and owned a home. However, she felt stuck in her career and desired a different path and therefore decided to study industrial psychology, a career change she knew would require a significant investment of hours and money to pursue.

Karen had no idea how she could make her finances work to support her new career goals. She didn't think she would be academically successful if she worked while she went back to school, but she also felt she didn't have enough financial resources to go to school without also working.

By changing her financial plan, Karen was able to go back to school and pursue her dream. She refinanced her mortgage, drastically cut her expenses, and maximized her savings until she gradually cut back her hours and started school. By being flexible, increasing her savings, and allowing herself the grace to see the transition as an opportunity despite the temporary impact it would have on her finances, Karen was able to go back to school while maintaining her financial independence.

HOW LIFESTYLE CREEP CAN IMPACT CAREER CHANGES

Unfortunately, we occasionally work with clients who let lifestyle creep negatively impact their financial decisions, preventing them from being flexible, building effective margins, or making graceful decisions.

We worked with Max and Jenny when they returned to the United States with their three kids after working overseas for several years. Max was an executive with a large company and made a good income. Overseas, their kids attended private school. When they returned to the states, Max and Jenny enrolled them in another private school and, despite our advice, decided to buy an extremely large and expensive house that they couldn't afford. Max was convinced that his company would do well and his stock options would provide the extra income needed to afford the house.

Unfortunately for Max and Jenny, the company did not perform to expectations. All of a sudden, their lifestyle, which was tied to a variable component—stock options—was really impacted.

JOB LOSS

Typically job loss negatively impacts a person's finances. This type of career transition is often unplanned and financially challenging.

CLIENT STORY
Between a Rock and Hard Place

My clients, Alice and Tom, owned a staffing business. It was lucrative and offered them a powerful way to save annually. In terms of making money, Alice and Tom had just hit their prime earning years when we began working together. Their business was growing, they were saving, they felt good about their finances, and they anticipated working and saving for another ten years.

One of Alice's key values was security. Tom, on the other hand, was a little more of a risk taker. They developed a retirement plan that leaned heavily on Alice's desire to save by maximizing 401(k) contributions and cash savings. They had a great plan in place, but then they hit an unexpected career change.

The country went into a recession, forcing the big companies Alice and Tom worked with to rapidly cut costs, thereby minimizing Tom and Alice's role as staffing providers.

Suddenly, the vendors Alice and Tom had developed strong relationships with had either been laid off or forced to retire, impacting the direct channels Alice and Tom had with the companies that kept their business afloat. This change drove down their revenues, which eventually caused them to get out of the staffing business altogether. This transition forced Alice and Tom, who had already made a solid retirement plan, to rethink their spending and retirement plans.

Alice and Tom would eventually make their finances work, but the transitional period was stressful for them both, as was the need to rethink their retirement vision.

SCALING BACK WORKING HOURS

One way to plan for retirement is by scaling back your working hours. This is a nice transition for those who are planning to gradually retire. When planned for effectively, this type of transition can be a great segue to retirement.

DISABILITY

With fifty-four million Americans living with a disability, it is not uncommon for people to experience a life transition because of a disability, whether that disability is work related or not.[35] As with any life transition, particularly unplanned ones, disabilities can affect lifestyle, emotional state, how people view themselves, and decision-making capabilities.

I worked with a couple who developed a financial plan that would pay for their high-school-aged kids' college tuition. However, the wife, who was a surgeon, developed a debilitating case of arthritis. This interfered with her ability to do surgery and forced her to spend more time doing clinical work. Her income, which was once stable and significant, not only decreased but also became volatile because it depended on the case work that came into the clinic. This disability—unexpected and work related—impacted their family's lifestyle and their ability to pay for their children's college educations.

---

35   Cornell University, "Disability Statistics," http://www.disabilitystatistics.org/faq.
cfm#Q9.

CLIENT STORY
Money Isn't Everything

Ben was a successful medical professional when he came to Flourish. Ben, who was in his early fifties, was making a good living, but his financials didn't match up with what we would normally expect for a doctor at that stage of his career. For example, he still had a sizeable amount of student loan debt.

This was an opportunity to dig into Ben's money history and money story. It turned out that he came to a realization in his mid-thirties that his successful career in IT wasn't making him happy. He found it unfulfilling and wanted to go back to school to become a doctor. Unlike Karen, the engineer, Ben hadn't saved well and didn't have many assets that could help sustain him during medical school. Knowing this, Ben decided to pursue medical school anyway because he found that helping others was a more important priority than earning income. Ben's career change would cause him to work ten years longer than his retirement plan had originally called for. These extra ten years of work meant nothing to Ben, who said he'd rather work ten more years doing something he loved than retire early doing something that didn't align with his values.

Inheritance

The one transition that really has the ability to change people's trajectory in terms of what they thought was possible in their life is inheritance. Inheritance can make many things—retirement, putting kids through college, paying off debt, traveling—feasible. It's like getting a job that you never thought was possible. It affects how you can spend, save, and invest money, and also how you might spend your time. It can also come with sadness with the loss of a loved one.

Housing

As are all aspects of your financial well-being, housing is affected by life transitions. When you lose a job, change your family situation, or get ready for retirement, understand that your housing situation may change. Often, retirees who are grandparents choose to relocate closer to their children and grandchildren. Therefore, it may be necessary to downsize, sell, review your mortgage, or, in some cases, buy a larger property.

Sometimes, clients fail to really look at their available housing resources and are, instead, optimistic that wherever they choose to live, they'll "make it work." One of my clients, Vicki, ended up getting a divorce. During the divorce, Vicki was adamant that she wanted to keep the family lake house. But after looking at her finances, she couldn't afford the expenses of the lake house while also living in her current home. However, the lake house was so important to her that she committed to selling her current home and living at the lake house year-round. The lake house was in the middle of Wisconsin. Going to a Wisconsin lake house in the summer when everybody is vacationing is a different experience than it is in the winter when it's cold and no one is around. When Vicki moved to the lake house, she was sad and lonely. She ended up selling it and renting a place closer to her family. It was really emotional for her. She wanted to keep the house in the family, yet keeping it didn't work with her long-term lifestyle and overall finances.

How to Survive Transitions

My most impactful work is accomplished when clients are in the midst of navigating life's major transitions. I can empathize with the difficulty of making good financial decisions during these periods of transition; I have experienced many of life's transitions myself. I have been divorced, gone through career changes, am in the process of raising a blended family, and have worked through family health issues with my parents. After experiencing several of my own transitions, I've discovered three coping mechanisms that make surviving a transition much easier: resilience, reserves, and respect.

RESILIENCE

When I left my former firm to start Flourish, I had no choice but to sever some relationships with clients I had previously worked with. I also had to tell my former company that I was leaving. This was difficult because I enjoyed my coworkers and personally cared about my clients and their families. We've all heard that death and taxes are life's only guarantees, but change is also one of life's only guarantees. The only effective balance to change is resilience, and one of the most effective ways to embrace change is by focusing on the positives.

Resiliency allowed us to move forward after our initial reactions of anger, sadness, and fear when Jay lost his job. By staying resilient, we were able to look at his job situation differently. This, in turn, led him to transition into a position at our company, Flourish.

THE RIGHT PLAN IS BETTER THAN A GOOD PLAN

We all build financial plans based on different assumptions. We assume spending will always be W, our healthcare needs will be X, our Social Security allotment will be Y, and we'll live for Z years. But what happens to our plans when any one of those assumptions change? The good plan that we had yesterday is no longer appropriate.

As soon as you create a financial plan, it's important to understand that it isn't a permanent plan because variables constantly change. The government may issue new tax rules, you might lose your job, or the country might hit a recession derailing every good intention you had to save and invest for retirement. This is why your plan must be flexible and resilient.

RESERVES

Major life transitions can require a lot of time and money, particularly in the early stages. It's almost impossible to effectively budget for the financial impact of a major life transition because they are all different. Even in situations where the type of transition is the same, such as divorce, the details involved are unique to each instance.

Knowing that transitions are inevitable and, while they tend to happen unexpectedly, are an expected part of life—and that even the best projections will most likely underestimate the true costs in time and money—we suggest building a reserve. A financial buffer will provide the money necessary to effectively work through the transition and, hopefully, provide some additional flexibility for time. Reserves can be a lifeline during a big transition, so we design retirement plans that include conservative assumptions such as the following:

- You should expect that most plans will take longer and cost more than expected.

- You should assume a life expectancy of ninety-five years or even longer depending on genetics rather than planning for average life expectancy. Depending on your age, you should reduce your reliance on the projected amount of Social Security.

- You should assume expenses at retirement may increase due to newfound pastimes or the ability to travel, and then decrease as lifestyle slows down, and then go up again to support additional medical expenses later in life.

- You should test the model to show what happens if one partner dies early, if additional expenses are incurred to support family members, and to project long-term care needs.

RESPECT

The changes and surprises that accompany life's transitions may feel like failures, at least initially. Jay's feelings of shame over his job loss came from feelings of failure. The reason he moved from a place of failure to success is because he allowed himself the opportunity to respect the transitional period without losing his self-respect. He eventually allowed himself to see the opportunities the change would offer, focusing on the opportunities ahead of him on the other side of the transition.

Allowing for resilience, reserves, and respect during career and financial transitions helps us to not only survive the transitions but to thrive because of them.

How to Manage Transitional Stress

"The secret of change is to focus all of your energy, not on fighting the old, but on building the new." — Socrates

Transitions are overwhelming. They take a mental and emotional toll on all of us, which is why it's important to honor the feelings you experience while going through a transition. Time and emotional support help provide perspective, creating the presence of mind to help clarify next steps. I've found that acceptance, reflection, living in the moment, consulting a mentor, practicing optimism, and looking for opportunities can help us all cope with transitions.

ACCEPTANCE

It's often difficult to accept the change that comes with any major transition because human nature fights things that are uncomfortable or unfamiliar. Whether you are experiencing the loss of a loved one, a major career change, a big move, or a divorce, accepting your new situation is an important step in making space for setting new goals and making new life decisions.

REFLECTION

Taking stock of who you really are and what you really want can have a lasting impact on the way you manage transitions. Self-reflection helps identify your main sources of challenge and worry. It also highlights the other side to any situation. Practicing meditation or yoga, talking with a therapist, journaling, or walking can help facilitate reflection and mindfulness.

LIVING IN THE MOMENT

During periods of transition we often look to the past or future for answers, comfort, or diversion. Yet the current moment—the one we are in—is the one that matters the most. It is what will move us toward our future. Setting small, attainable goals for the future makes challenges seem more manageable.

CONSULTING A MENTOR

Whether it's a friend, colleague, coach, parent, sibling, or advisor, having a confidant to share your thoughts, concerns, ideas, and options with can be of great benefit when you are in the throes of a major life change. Mentors provide a great source for clarity and outlet for your thoughts.

PRACTICING OPTIMISM

When things are tumultuous, having a negative outlook can be easier than having a positive one. However, optimism is a skill that can be honed like a great golf swing or an expert soufflé. If you can overcome negative thought patterns and cultivate a positive outlook, it will shift your mindset to one of opportunity rather than challenge. Every transition, though often tiresome, has something beneficial to bring to your life.

LOOKING FOR OPPORTUNITIES

The Sherpas of Nepal spend their days guiding eager, daring travelers up the treacherous paths of Mount Everest and other Himalayan peaks. What they witness in a month is likely more terrifying than what most of us have experienced in a lifetime. And yet, they continue guiding thousands of visitors per year. I admire these Sherpas because they embrace the uncertainty that the Himalayas hold as part of their life and their livelihood.

When it comes to major transitions in our own lives, take a lesson from the Sherpas. They do not seek to remove themselves from the challenges they face. Rather, they find the most navigable solution in order to arrive safely on the other side of the mountain. They look for opportunities when others assume there are none.

In our society we are encouraged to look at things in black and white. Did we succeed, or did we fail? During transitions, this mentality can hinder our ability to see a new path or beginning. It can stop us from envisioning something new for ourselves and from taking the steps necessary to make that potential a reality. When going through a transition, understand that your experiences are opportunities to learn and grow. Looking at your circumstances through a new lens will help you ask the right questions that will allow you to discover what could be.

Understanding that life transitions are things that we must get through, not out of, is a great step in the process of breaking down what needs to be done in order to come through the storm and continue on our journey to the summit.

Conversation Starters

1. If you went through an unexpected career transition today, how long could you live off your savings? How would a career or financial transition impact your retirement plan?

2. How would it impact your housing situation?

3. How could you change your retirement plan to adjust to one of these transitions?

4. How does your financial plan incorporate emergency reserves?

5. How have you successfully navigated transitions in the past?

6. What transitions are you most looking forward to in life?

7. What transitions, if any, are you not looking forward to?

CHAPTER 5

What to Expect When You're Expecting the Unexpected: The Reality of Marriage, Kids, and Even Divorce

I'm adopted. I gave birth to my oldest daughter, Maddy, when I was with my ex-husband. My second (and final) husband Jay and I adopted our son, Fernando, and our youngest daughter, Grace, from Guatemala. Fifty years ago, our family may have been atypical. Today, it's just one of many newer, but increasingly common, familial structures.

My family also reflects multiple transitions. I've personally experienced adoption along with the transitions of marriage, having a child, divorce, a second marriage, and more adoptions. Most of these transitions were conscious, deliberate decisions, but some were unexpected. Hopefully my personal experience with transitions, along with my efforts to help many clients over the years, can provide helpful perspective to help you navigate through family transitions you may face in life.

Marriage

Marriage is a wonderful, special transition that, for many people, happens more than once. No matter what your marriage looks like, having a money conversation with your new spouse can be complex. You each bring your own money story, values, and financial resources and obligations to the relationship.

While money certainly allows us to live a certain lifestyle, when two people come into a marriage with separate money values it can create complications. Here are six ways to ensure that money doesn't cause your breakup.

1. COMMIT TO MARRIAGE WITH EYES WIDE OPEN.

Before you marry, gather your financial history including a summary of your assets, liabilities, income, spending, and individual credit report histories. Knowing where you both stand financially will help ease future financial tensions and misunderstandings.

2. COMMUNICATE.

Share your money history so your spouse can understand how the messages you have received about money have impacted your long-term money values. This also creates a foundation for future money conversations.

3. SET GOALS.

Share both short- and long-term goals with your spouse, including the financial components of each goal. Having a goals conversation will help clarify joint spending decisions and help you each understand wants versus needs.

4. DEVELOP GOOD MECHANICS.

Consider how expenses will be treated. Will expenses be combined and paid from one account, or will you have a household account and separate accounts for individual expenses? Should household expenses be shared equally, or should there be another method based on each spouse's share of the income?

5. WORK TOGETHER.

Busy couples often defer most of the financial decisions to one person, but both spouses need to remain engaged. That includes regular update conversations including updates on progress toward short- and long-term goals.

6. KEEP COMMUNICATING.

This last point is critical. As we talked about in chapter 4, the transitional factors affecting your finances are constantly in flux. The economy, a change in your industry, or a turn in your health or the health of someone you love can dramatically affect your finances. They can also affect your and/or your spouse's attitude toward money.

CLIENT STORY
Butting Heads

I worked with one couple that couldn't come together on an investment plan, in large part because of their refusal to communicate. The husband felt there was no upside left in the stock market, so he put all of their savings in cash. His wife didn't think that decision was a viable way to plan for retirement or college savings for their kids. It was a source of tension that was triggered by their different risk tolerances and a lack of communication. Had the husband agreed to keep talking about potential solutions, they might have reached a compromise that suited both of their values and goals.

TOP MONEY DISCUSSIONS DIVORCED COUPLES SAY NEWLYWEDS SHOULD HAVE[36]

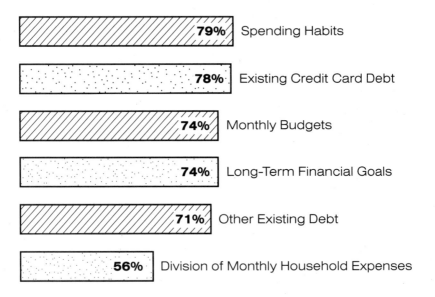

79% Spending Habits

78% Existing Credit Card Debt

74% Monthly Budgets

74% Long-Term Financial Goals

71% Other Existing Debt

56% Division of Monthly Household Expenses

36 "Nearly Half of Divorced or Separated US Adults Wish They Had Spent More Time Discussing Finances Before Marriage, Finds New CouponCabin.com Survey," CouponCabin, accessed through Cision PR Newswire, (May 23, 2012): https://www.prnewswire.com/news-releases/nearly-half-of-divorced-or-separated-us-adults-wish-they-had-spent-more-time-discussing-finances-before-marriage-finds-new-couponcabincom-survey-152995905.html.

Divorce

It's a pleasure to share life's happy moments with our clients. However, we know not all events are cause for joy. Clients often seek our advice when they're going through challenging and difficult transitions such as divorce, a major life transition that impacts approximately half of all families. Divorce is one of the most challenging and stressful life events that a person can experience. Most of us don't plan for divorce. When it happens, nearly every aspect of life changes in an instant, which is devastating and can take a toll on your willpower and decision-making skills. Divorce is mentally and emotionally draining. It is also fraught with practicalities that must be addressed so that, when the dust settles, you find yourself standing on solid ground.

Divorce undermines a great deal of the financial planning and wealth building that a couple accomplished during marriage. However, those who let financial decisions slide while they're going through a divorce risk leaving their financial future in the hands of their ex-spouse. To avoid this situation, know what needs to be addressed today, what can wait, and which documents you'll need to make responsible decisions when you are ready to make them.

GIVE IT TIME

While it is important to stay on top of your finances throughout the divorce process, very few things need to happen overnight. As is the case with any transition, when you start going through a divorce, you need to be patient and not let your emotions redefine your financial future.

While time can help you make solid financial decisions during a divorce, there are a few things you want to do right away:

- Work through the emotions of divorce.

- Gather your financial information, making copies of tax returns, and statements.

- Understand your debt obligations. Even if your ex agrees to pay for certain debts, you are still responsible for them before the divorce is finalized if they are not paid.

- Accept that you might have to let go of your home. Many divorcees assume that they have to stay in the same home, which can cause serious financial issues.

DIVORCE AFTER FIFTY

According to a recent study, one in four divorces is initiated by couples over the age of fifty.[37] A study on the rising rates of divorce among older generations shows older divorcees have one fifth of the wealth of people who stay married. Because recovering from lost assets close to retirement is difficult, it's critical to find a way to end a marriage in a way that will protect as much of your net worth and financial resources as possible.

MAKE A LIST

A married couple often accumulates multiple banking, investment, insurance, and other financial accounts. Over time and during the trauma of a divorce, it can be hard to remember where the accounts are.

---

37 Wilkinson & Finkbeiner, "Everything You Need to Know about Divorce—Facts, Statistics, and Rates," http://www.wf-lawyers.com/divorce-statistics-and-facts/.

YOUR DIVORCE DOCUMENTS CHECKLIST

The following documents will help you get organized as you prepare for a divorce:

- bank and investment statements including details of investment holdings for all personal and retirement accounts
- tax returns for the last three years
- paystubs
- employee benefit information including stock options or employee stock purchase plans
- Social Security estimate of benefits
- statements for existing mortgages, lines of credit, credit cards, or other debt
- life insurance policies
- a copy of the tax records, assets, and debts of any businesses owned by the couple
- additional documents including deeds, prenuptial or antenuptial agreements, wills, health care directives, and financial powers of attorney

KEEP EMOTIONS OUT OF IT

One of the most effective ways to come out financially on top of a divorce is to keep emotions out of your decisions. After you've given things time, looked at the relevant documents, set your own financial priorities, accepted the changes in your life, and talked to a CDFA (see next section on working with a CDFA to learn more), you will be closer to making divorce-related financial decisions. Here are four steps for keeping those emotions at bay while making those decisions.

1. Keep records and plan ahead.

Divorce is a complicated process. It can be beneficial to consult with legal and financial professionals before you announce your intentions to divorce. You will need to have copies of tax returns, wills, trusts, financial statements, insurance policies, and deeds to property. All of these items will be necessary to determine how the finances will be divided and in what manner. Depending on how amicable your relationship is with your ex, these may be easy or difficult to retrieve after you start living apart.

2. Be assertive and aware.

Although it is important not to let heightened emotions get the better of you, it is also important to ensure that you get what you need and deserve out of the dissolution of your marriage. Having the means to take care of yourself, prepare for the next chapter of your life, and maintain a comparable standard of living is not vengeful; it is necessary and important. This requires having a healthy sense of control over the process, taking part in the negotiations, and not being a passive observer of your divorce.

3. Engage in the present and let go of the past.

There is an overwhelming rollercoaster of emotions that comes with divorce. Maintaining a strong connection with being in the current moment can help you manage feelings of anger, resentment, sadness, and loss.

4. Be mindful.

Mindfulness can help your subconscious release hard feelings and start to approach life with a "me" rather than a "we" mentality. Try not to think about "we." That leads to feelings of loss, grief, and a reminder that "we" has been dissolved. Having a good support network will help you to manage those feelings and channel them into new, positive experiences with others who love and care for you.

WORK WITH A CDFA

Certified Divorce Financial Analysts (CDFAs) are members of the Institute for Divorce Financial Analysts and are specially trained to help with the personal financial considerations throughout the divorce process.

Specifically, a CDFA[38] ...

- works with the divorce team to provide the client and lawyer with data that shows the financial effect of any given divorce settlement

- appears as an expert witness if the case goes to court, mediation, or arbitration

- is familiar with tax issues that apply to divorce

- has background knowledge of the legal issues in divorce

- helps clients identify their future financial goals, develop a budget, identify which kind of lifestyle they want, identify their insurance needs, and set retirement objectives

- identifies the short-term and long-term effects of dividing property

- integrates tax issues

- analyzes pension and retirement plan issues

- determines if the client can afford the matrimonial home and, if not, what might be an affordable alternative, and

- brings an innovative and creative approach to settling cases.

---

38   "What Is a CFDA Professional?" Institute for Divorce Financial Analysts, January 29, 2013, https://institutedfa.com/learning-center/what-cdfa-professional/.

STEPS TO TAKE AFTER THE DIVORCE

After the divorce, use your divorce decree to make a physical list of the accounts that you have been awarded in your settlement so you can start changing the account ownership. Be sure to include any insurance policies. Insurance policies are often forgotten, but they're important as they will allow you to provide for children or other dependents after you pass away. Sometimes, divorcees will inadvertently leave their ex as the beneficiary of life insurance policies and retirement accounts, creating surprises and undue hardship for the intended beneficiaries when the proceeds go to a former spouse.

Review any legal documents that you signed with an ex-spouse during your marriage. This can include documents related to health care and end-of-life decisions such as powers of attorney or living wills. Although rules about whether the documents remain valid after divorce vary by state, the best process is to revoke old powers of attorney and living wills and replace them with updated agreements, naming new individuals to act on your behalf for these critical decisions. Share the updated documents with the named individuals in your documents so they have the information on file and are fully aware of your future plans.

Set Your Priorities and Yours Only

There are opportunities in divorce. Whereas you may have had to compromise before, divorce allows you to manage your personal relationships and your financial legacy in a way that matches your values and goals. For example, you can include a charity in legacy planning that might not have been a shared priority during the marriage.

When you start post-divorce planning, decide what you'd like to do differently with your financial assets. Also, consider which existing priorities you want to maintain. While providing financial support to children or grandchildren for higher education may have been a priority when you were married, it might change during divorce. Sometimes, it's easier for two people to accomplish financial goals than it is for one person, so you may have to adjust your plan to reflect your new financial situation.

Setting these priorities can be overwhelming, so try to focus on two things:

1. setting your big-picture goals before getting into the financial minutiae necessary to achieve these goals, and

2. considering how today's decisions will affect your future financial stability.

Prepare for Change

Your life may take a different, unexpected turn after divorce. Getting remarried might change how assets are distributed to your children from your earlier marriage, especially if you're adding stepchildren to the mix. It is important to take control of the process by creating a strong estate plan to ensure that your assets follow the path you intended.

After updating your documents, a regular review of your estate plan should happen every three to five years. As you add new relationships, you may discover the need to update this plan more frequently.

Prepare for a New Lifestyle

Regardless of whether you remarry, most divorce leads to a change in lifestyle, even if that change is only temporary. For most people, divorce requires some paring down of lifestyle. It means paying your own insurance premiums, utility bills, and mortgage on half or less than half of the income you previously enjoyed.

My clients who view divorce as an opportunity to pursue a lifestyle that wasn't possible before eventually end up enjoying their post-divorce life. My client Sue got divorced because she didn't feel connected to her husband. They didn't share the same interests or goals in life. Once they divorced, Sue moved out of state, started traveling more, and pursued her interest in the arts. She rethought her own life and, as a result, got to experience things she couldn't experience during her marriage.

Visualize the Post-Divorce Lifestyle You Will Lead

To determine what your post-divorce lifestyle might look like, ask yourself the following:

1. What type of lifestyle do I want and is it realistic based on my assets and likely settlement?

2. How much income will I need to live the lifestyle I desire?

3. Where will I live?

4. If I'm divorcing after fifty, and haven't worked outside the home for many years, will I go back to work? If so, will I need training, how long will that take, and how much am I likely to earn when I reenter the workforce?

5. When will I want to retire or need to start tapping into savings?

6. What are my goals for the kids? What unique needs should be considered?

7. Will I want or need to leave money to my children or grandchildren?

8. Will I want to donate to charitable organizations?

Kids

Sometimes, when we think about the possibility of having children, we are so consumed by our desire to have a family and the excitement of watching those children grow that we forget to think about the financial considerations associated with raising a family.

Divorce, adoption, caring for children with special needs, planning for college, and transitioning from a full house to an empty nest all carry financial implications that require some planning.

BLENDED FAMILIES

As tough as financial conversations can be for newlyweds, they're doubly complicated for those of us who have been married more than once. This complexity only increases with blended families. I've found from first-hand experience as well as working with clients that blended families need additional planning to prepare for various life stages. The following questions will help facilitate important financial planning conversations.

What Are Your Obligations and Resources?

A couple that has a blended family needs to have a clear understanding of the obligations and resources that each parent brings to the marriage. Obligations can include child support and spousal maintenance, in addition to any outstanding debts. Resources can include the assets each person brings to the relationship, amounts saved for college, and, of course, child support.

What Standard of Living Is Expected?

Children of blended families may join the blended family with different standards of living based on their parents' values and financial resources. We're talking about some big dollars when it comes to kids and spending. The average cost for a middle-income family to raise a child born in 2015 to the age of eighteen has increased to $233,610 according to the latest report from the US Department of Agriculture. Those numbers are astounding, as this doesn't even include college cost.[39] It is important for blended families to begin talking about the expected standard of living within the shared household, early. I have noted many cases where resentment and frustration build when couples haven't established this understanding, or when their values clash when it comes to decide what to spend on each child.

One family may believe in giving allowances while another may believe that kids should get a job to pay for their own spending. Another may value public education while yet another may value private schooling. Jay and I ran into this challenge when Maddy was five. I grew up going to Catholic school; Jay went to public schools. When it was time for Maddy to attend school, I preferred a (private) Catholic school. Our public schools were facing budget cuts, so I thought Catholic school would provide a better education. Jay disagreed. After much discussion, we sent Maddy to public school. After a couple years the public school started to have financial issues and Maddy actually lost a really good teacher due to budget cuts. We agreed to move her to a Catholic school where she earned a great education and Jay and I resolved our differences. We were fortunate that my ex-husband deferred to my decision about where Maddy went to school, but that can be a source of contention in some blended families.

When Jay and I married, I didn't anticipate the financial decisions we would have to make together to meet Maddy's monetary needs, or the impact two sets of parents would have on making those choices. I also didn't anticipate how often we'd have to have conversations with

---

39 Mark Lino, "The Cost of Raising a Child," USDA Media Blog, (Jan. 13, 2017): https://www.usda.gov/media/blog/2017/01/13/cost-raising-child.

my ex-husband about spending for Maddy. As kids age, how their parents spend money on them also changes. Every phase seems to bring a new spending challenge for blended families. For example, when kids start driving, it leads to conversations about whether they get a car and who pays for insurance, gas, and the vehicle. We faced this challenge when Maddy turned sixteen.

When your kids start driving and then when they turn eighteen, bigger spending decisions come to the forefront. Who should pay for college? What percentage of college will be paid for by each parent? Do certain expectations (grades, for instance) need to be achieved for payments to continue? Oftentimes, our values in terms of college funding are influenced by our own experience and how our own higher education was funded. Some parents believe their kids should pay a portion of their college expenses and have a stake in the financial responsibility of going to school, while others feel that a college education is something parents should provide to their children.

Additional considerations such as whether children work, whether it's all right to borrow funds for college, or whether they'll attend a public or private university must also be considered. For blended families, even the financial aid process becomes more complex than it does for other families because stepparents' income is included in financial aid calculations along with that of the custodial parent, making it more difficult to qualify for assistance, even if the family unit with a higher income doesn't meaningfully contribute to the college costs.

What Happens When You Die?

Blended families bring another set of challenges when it comes to estate planning: the "his, hers, and ours" conundrum. The needs of both spouses and their children must be considered for passing on assets. This can lead to misunderstandings and hurt feelings. For instance, a spouse might have a desire to provide for the other spouse but, ultimately, wants to ensure that their assets pass to their children.

There are structures and trust planning strategies that can be established to ensure assets, ultimately, go to the kids, while also benefiting the spouse while he or she is still living. But how does it feel for the kids from a first marriage to wait another twenty years while assets are locked in a trust for their stepparent? Sometimes, it makes sense to provide for the children in some fashion when the first spouse passes away, whether this is a gift or even designated assets (such as proceeds from a life insurance policy).

CLIENT STORY
Preparing for Your Unique Situation

I worked with one blended family that had children from prior marriages that were of different ages. The wife was about fifteen years younger than the husband, and her two children were in grade school while the husband's kids were in college. Both spouses came into the marriage with a good amount of financial resources, so they wanted to create an estate plan to accomplish two goals: (1) support spending for the surviving spouse in the event of one of their deaths, and (2) pass their personal assets to their respective biological children. They also wanted to create a solution where the surviving spouse wouldn't feel awkward about spending part of the estate or have kids waiting for them to die so they could gain an inheritance. The couple decided to give a specific gift for each child after first parental death and then place the rest of their assets in a trust for the benefit of the remaining spouse, which would ultimately pass to their respective biological kids.

It's important to consider the ex-spouse while estate planning. Is your ex-spouse entitled to anything when you pass? Will your ex-spouse leave the kids anything? If so, how will that impact your estate planning goals? For example, if your ex-spouse is leaving a $500,000 legacy for your child that might impact your planning decisions.

CARING FOR KIDS WITH SPECIAL NEEDS

Caring for children with special needs requires financial planning that is more extensive than planning for children who do not have special needs. Parents who have children with special needs spend an average of $326 per month, or just under $4,000 per year, on out-of-pocket medical expenses for their child.[40] Not only do these parents have more medical bills than other families, they also may have to consider how these children are financially cared for throughout their adult lives.

---

40 M & L Special Needs Planning, "Statistics: Reasons for Special Needs Financial life Plans," http://specialneedsplanning.net/statistics/.

Facts about Children with Special Needs[41]

Twenty percent of Americans between the ages of sixteen and sixty-four suffer some form of physical, mental, or emotional impairment. Many of them are outliving their parents thanks to improved care and medical technology.

Eighty-eight percent of parents who have children with special needs have not set up a trust to preserve eligibility for benefits such as Medicaid and Supplemental Security Income.

Thirty-two percent of parents with special needs children spend more than forty hours per week with their special needs child, which is equal to a second full-time job.

---

41 Ibid.

ADOPTION

In 2013 and 2014, the average adoption cost fell between $34,093 and $39,966.[42] In addition to being costly, adoptions are not always guaranteed. This is a very personal topic, as I was adopted as a baby, and our youngest two children, Fernando and Grace, are both adopted from Guatemala. I've been fortunate to be part of three successful adoption stories, and am proud of the role adoption has played in our family. However, for those considering adoption, it is important to fully understand and incorporate the additional expenses into your financial plan.

PLANNING FOR COLLEGE

In terms of priorities, retirement savings generally always come before saving for college. Once you have a pool of retirement dollars and a plan for sustaining your income and lifestyle during retirement, then you can consider what you can really afford to pay for college.

If it's an option to pay for college from current cash flow without sacrificing your lifestyle or retirement plan, those parents will come into "newfound" money again when those kids graduate.

NURTURING THE EMPTY NEST

When your children leave home for the first time, the transition to having an empty house can be challenging. It can also be very exciting! Similar to retirement, divorce, or any life transition, the range of emotions can vary, and how you manage your time, feelings, finances, and relationships through that transition can have an impact on your well-being and lifestyle.

---

42 American Adoptions, "Comparing the Costs of Domestic, International and Foster Care Adoption," http://www.americanadoptions.com/adopt/the_costs_of_adopting.

Top Tips for Empty Nesters

1. *Revisit your financial plan.*

Be aware that many of the assumptions underlying your current financial plan may be obsolete. College tuition payments may be completed. You might have more living space than you need or want. You have more time to travel and pursue hobbies. Spend time thinking about what you'd like to do after the kids leave and how you will fund that plan.

2. *Plan for retirement.*

When the kids leave, it's a great time to straighten out your retirement plan. First, create a list of financial goals to focus on. Many empty-nesters focus on paying off outstanding debts, such as their mortgage, to reduce monthly expenses. Others choose to increase retirement account savings before they have to start withdrawing from those accounts. Then, break down your finances as they currently stand and see where your spending can be adjusted to help you save or pay off debt.

3. *Focus on you.*

After parents have cared for children for many years, an empty nest provides them with an opportunity to focus on themselves. While this can evoke feelings of discomfort, it can also lead to rediscovering the things that bring happiness beyond being a parent and caregiver. Having a plan to make these discoveries can help you feel more comfortable with your newly found free time.

The Come Back Kid

The interesting thing about today's empty nest is that it doesn't always remain empty. According to the Bureau of Labor Statistics, 90 percent of children have moved out of their parents' house for at least a three-month period by the time they are twenty-seven, with a median move-out age of nineteen.[43] Interestingly, 54.6 percent of those who moved out of their parents' home moved back in for a period of time before they were twenty-seven.[44]

Living Arrangements of Eighteen- to Thirty-Four-Year-Olds Over Time

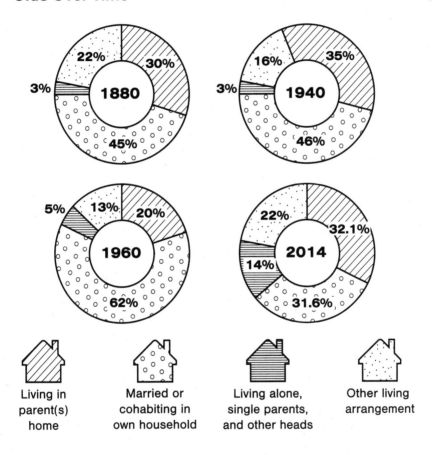

Living in parent(s) home

Married or cohabiting in own household

Living alone, single parents, and other heads

Other living arrangement

---

43 Bureau of Labor Statistics, "Independence for Young Millennials: Moving Out and Boomeranging Back," (December 2014): https://www.bls.gov/opub/mlr/2014/article/independence-for-young-millennials-moving-out-and-boomeranging-back.htm.

44 Ibid.

I see these "boomerang" kids all the time. They return to Mom and Dad's house while looking for work, saving money to buy a house, or finishing their education. Many of my clients open their homes back up to their children but fail to think how their expenses change when they do so.

When you're starting your empty nest lifestyle, consider whether you can afford to cover the cost of an extra person living under your roof again should one or more of your children choose to move back in. It's important to determine whether you should charge them rent to help keep your own expenses down or to convey the message that they need to contribute to the home in which they live.

I've observed parents who supplement the incomes of their boomerang kids to their own detriment. My client Mae had some investment assets and a lot of equity in her house. However, she was living with her son who wasn't paying rent. Mae really struggled to charge her forty-five-year-old son rent. Her attitude was, "Well, he's helpful to have around the house." Yet she was spending most of her assets to support the house and him. Eventually, this added financial burden forced Mae to consider looking for ways to access her home equity. She simply didn't want to say no to her son and make him contribute to the household expenses.

If your kid(s) return, develop a plan that will work for everyone. It might be a tapering effect where you agree to help them for so long but will start charging rent at a certain point, with the understanding that they move out by a predetermined date. Setting deadlines will help them reconfigure their timeline and understand what the consequences will be for failing to meet a deadline. As much as you want to help your children, helping them should not threaten your own financial security.

While you're thinking about how a boomerang kid might impact your finances, also consider what might happen to your financial plan if you and/or your spouse end up caring for one or both sets of your parents.

Other clients I've advised included a couple who married a little later in life. They both had good jobs, but all of a sudden, both of their parents needed care. The wife had a higher-paying job, so the husband stopped working to care for both sets of parents. He took them to the doctor and managed their finances while his wife kept working and maximizing their retirement savings. If they had not had a plan for how to manage retirement funds while also caring for their parents, he most certainly couldn't have stopped working to care for them.

I have lived through a divorce, a second marriage, am raising a blended family, and am in the process of sending my oldest child to college. Life transitions are difficult! They are joyful, disappointing, exciting—and often unpredictable. But there are ways to plan for them that can help smooth even the toughest of transitions.

Conversation Starters

1. What key financial conversations will you have with your fiancé before the wedding day?

2. Who can help you get your financial documents in order as you go through your divorce?

3. What post-divorce lifestyle do you envision?

4. If you're starting a blended family, where will the children live, who will pay for their education and medical treatment, who will pay for their schooling, and what happens when you or your spouse dies?

5. How will you change your financial plan when your children leave home?

6. What financial expectations will you set for a boomerang child?

7. How might your kids or parents impact your long-term financial plan?

CHAPTER 6

Retirement at Face Value: Finding Joy and Confidence in Retirement Planning

The transition from working full time to retirement raises all types of emotions. There's the excitement that, after decades of hard, diligent work, your time is all your own. But are you apprehensive at the thought of having to fill those forty hours? Or, are you experiencing fear because your savings are less than you expected? Or perhaps you're feeling sadness and emptiness because the career that defined you is now over.

The great retirement paradox is that there is so much time, and yet so very little of it. Yes, we are living longer, healthier lives, yet at some point it will come to an end. So what do we do with this new chapter of life that may last another twenty or thirty years? While that thirty-year horizon is full of possibilities, it can also be daunting and full of questions: Did I save enough? How will I spend my time? Where will I live? What kind of legacy will I leave?

Understand How Retirement Might Affect You Emotionally

I often work with clients who struggle with the discomfort of being newly retired. This struggle occurs in those who haven't given enough thought to what their life might look like when they leave their career. The challenges might be associated with identity, relationships, finding new ways to fill time, or maintaining frequent social interaction.

The money emotions we talked about in chapter 1—excitement, fear, responsibility, and sadness—are likely to resurface during retirement. There's the excitement of closing one of life's chapters and starting another. For those who have planned what they want to do during retirement, there's the excitement of spending their time doing what they truly enjoy. With that excitement comes a bit of fear. Some fear turning off their paychecks in retirement. There's the fear that if the unexpected does happen, it will be more difficult to find a job. There's the fear of running out of money or encountering an unplanned sickness or other large expense. The sadness comes from the same place as the excitement: knowing you're closing one chapter of your life and starting another. You feel the responsibility for filling an unknown amount of time with a finite amount of resources, and hope you've planned well enough.

Whatever the struggle, if you ask yourself tough questions about retirement and develop a plan for how you want to live during retirement *before* you retire, your chances of feeling empowered, excited, and accomplished when beginning retirement will be much greater than if you don't think before you leap.

WHO AM I?

Most adults spend much of their life identifying themselves as a professional or as a parent or both. By the time they reach retirement age, their children have flown the coop (hopefully) and they are about to leave what might be the strongest connection to their personal identity: their job.

In order to cope with this adjustment, individuals need to discover their new retirement identity. Getting an "identity makeover" can be challenging, but it's also extremely valuable. First, consider things beyond work and your children that bring you a sense of purpose and independence. For some, this may be playing a more active role as a grandparent or spouse, becoming a mentor, or participating in their community or local government. For others, this may mean starting a second or encore career or traveling. Taking time to think about a new retirement identity will help you enjoy your newfound time and freedom.

YOU ARE NOT YOUR HOBBIES

I hear many people, men in particular, say, "Oh I'll be fine with all the time I'll have in retirement. I can turn off work. I love to golf. I've got plenty to do." I don't know anyone who golfs seven days a week, twelve hours a day. I recommend that clients who are prone to rely on a hobby to fill their retirement time use a calendar to map out how they might spend their time. What would their mornings look like? What would their afternoons look like? What kind of evening routines would they develop? I try to get them to envision how they will spend the bulk of their time so they can see where they might have significant amounts of time to fill.

WHO AM I LIVING WITH?

Retirement generally means spending more time with your spouse, which can be challenging. The most common factors that contribute to added marital strain postretirement are the timing of the retirement, how closely the retiree's identity is intertwined with work, the couple's roles within the relationship, and competing retirement goals.

Thirty-eight percent of couples who aren't yet retired disagree about the lifestyle they expect to live in retirement, and one in three couples disagree as to their ideal vision for retirement.[45] Research shows that fostering conversations about retirement is a powerful tool to help people visualize a satisfying and fulfilling retirement lifestyle. After all, it's much easier to establish a plan of action when both spouses have shared a clear picture of their retirement vision.

I recommend that couples communicate well in advance of the actual retirement date to set ground rules and make plans. We have many clients who are very happy in their marriages after retirement and most, if not all, of them are very clear about two things: (1) when they will retire, and (2) how they will spend time together and apart. Being proactive about how you'll spend time together and what you expect out of each other's behavior might ease the tensions that can arise when one or both spouses prepare to retire.

Identify Your Ideal Retirement Lifestyle

When considering what your retirement plans might be, do a realistic self-assessment of what you like about your career and what you might lose when you retire. This can really help highlight some of

---

45   Fidelity Investments, "2013 Couples Retirement Study Executive Summary," https://www.fidelity.com/static/dcle/welcome/documents/CouplesRetirementStudy.pdf.

the activities you might want to pursue when you retire. This exercise may also inspire creative ideas for filling time that you haven't considered before.

If you think about it, activities such as traveling and spending more time with family are typically over shorter periods of time. You may spend the weekend with old friends, or a week with the grandkids, but you can't overlook the forty hours you have to fill most weeks. Is there something about your community that you'd like to see change? Do you see an opportunity where you could teach people a skill? Is there a group or a person that you'd like to help? Do you have a hobby that, with enough time, could become a small business? What aspects of your job will you miss, and are there ways to continue to perform them in a different capacity once you leave?

Answering these types of questions will help identify opportunities to fill your time with substantive activities and experiences with a sense of purpose. It will also help determine the financial resources you'll need to live your retirement lifestyle.

CLIENT STORY
Barking Up the Right Tree

One client who was nearing retirement really wanted to travel, but we discovered that extensive travel over several years wouldn't be realistic when we looked at her retirement plan. Then this client came across Rover, an online company that pairs pet owners with pet and house sitters. She decided that she would fund her travels by becoming a Rover sitter. She got paid to house and pet sit while also getting to stay in a house, city, or area she wanted to see.

STAY ACTIVE

Discovering your retirement identity can play a beneficial role in helping you choose how to remain active and engaged in your day-to-day activities. According to a Georgia State University (GSU) study published in the *Journals of Gerontology*, those who worked part-time, volunteered, or otherwise spent their time in active and socially engaged situations in retirement had a lower likelihood of developing age-related chronic health conditions.[46]

If you have always enjoyed arranging flowers or gardening, get a part-time job at a florist's, or volunteer at a local greenhouse. If you were in IT and you still have a passion for technology, perhaps assist local businesses with network setups or volunteer at a school or community organization to teach others who are interested in IT.

Devote your retirement planning to finding a balance between enjoying the relaxation of retirement without becoming sedentary. As the GSU study shows, staying active is critical to your emotional and physical well-being.

THINK ABOUT HOUSING

Housing is one of those transitional items that come up time and time again. It has to be considered when jobs are lost, promotions are gained, when family dynamics change, and when retirement is planned for.

---

46 B. L. Kail, and D. C. Carr, "Successful Aging in the Context of the Disablement Process: Working and Volunteering as Moderators on the Association between Chronic Conditions and Subsequent Functional Limitations," Journals of Gerontology Series B 72, no. 2 (March 1, 2017): 340–350, doi: 10.1093/geronb/gbw060; also available at National Center for Biotechnology Information, https://www.ncbi.nlm.nih.gov/pubmed/27225973.

Home ownership is one of our largest expenses and, if it's not planned for, it can impact your retirement lifestyle. For some people, planning for transitional housing at the beginning of retirement is the most practical option. It gives them time to wear their new retirement identity before committing to any major change in housing. For those who want to travel, condos or townhomes—which have more support and resources than a single family home—might make more sense.

One piece of advice I will offer is that if you are planning to move when you retire, consider the market. I knew one woman who really wanted to move near her kids in Chicago when she retired. However, she lived in Minnesota while she was working and didn't factor in the major differences in the housing prices between suburban Minnesota and downtown Chicago. Unfortunately, when she retired, she realized she wouldn't be able to afford living in Chicago long-term.

Get Your Finances in Order

According to the 2017 PwC survey mentioned in the first chapter, fewer than half of baby boomers know how much income they will need in retirement and are concerned that they will run out of money.[47] That kind of uncertainty compounds the stress that many people often face when trying to save and prepare for retirement.

Visualizing your retirement is one way to give yourself peace of mind about how to achieve it. The following eight steps can help you create a successful and fruitful retirement plan.

---

47   Financial Stress and the Bottom Line, PWC, special report, https://www.pwc.com/ us/en/industries/private-company-services/library/financial-well-being-retirement-survey.html.

1. SET GOALS.

Setting a goal is about more than choosing an arbitrary number to shoot for. Your plan should consider your lifestyle and how much that lifestyle will cost. Also, be sure to consider any financial support you intend to provide to children or grandchildren while you are alive as well as anything you might like to leave in your estate plan.

2. CREATE A SPENDING PLAN.

Having a well-thought-out spending plan will help you establish financial goals and control your expenses. In addition to watching your spending and reducing debt, you need to create a way to replace your current income stream. This may be as simple as setting up your accounts so that when you retire, you receive a monthly "paycheck" that comes from your investment accounts rather than an employer. This often helps people who are used to getting and spending a paycheck stay within their budget.

3. SAVE.

Your spending plan and your savings plan need to work hand-in-hand. Obviously, you can only save money you don't spend. Building a prioritized line item for monthly savings directly into your budget will help you stay on track with your planning goals.

4. PLAN FOR SOCIAL SECURITY.

It would be a mistake not to give Social Security much thought until the day you make your filing decision. It is important to consider each claim option prior to deciding how and when to receive benefits. If you are married, it is even more important to plan ahead. The decisions you make about Social Security can negatively impact a surviving spouse in the event of your passing. Thinking about Social Security sooner rather than later can help you make a decision that will maximize your benefits and provide an added layer of protection as you age.

5. LOOK AT TAX PLANNING.

Many retirees find it difficult to determine which accounts to use for living expenses as there are various tax consequences depending on the type of account. At age seventy-and-a-half, you must begin taking withdrawals from your retirement accounts. If you plan to retire before reaching that age, strategically using retirement accounts earlier may help minimize taxes. Overall, it is important to come up with a tax-efficient plan to use your assets along with income sources such as Social Security.

6. CONSIDER THE LEGACY YOU WANT TO LEAVE.

In addition to developing spending and savings goals for retirement, some people want to leave money to children, grandchildren, or charities when they pass. These gifts are called "legacies," and should be considered in every retirement plan. If you want to leave $250,000 to each of your children, how you spend and save today will look different from what it will if you want to leave $10,000 to each of them. Although I've mentioned this before, it's worth mentioning again: you have to be comfortable that your needs will be met for your own retirement, and that you won't run out of money before you can think about leaving a legacy. At the same time, leaving a legacy isn't for everyone; I recently heard a client refer to their plans to travel in their retirement as taking "SKI Trips," which stands for "Spending Kids' Inheritance."

7. PACE YOURSELF.

Retirees often go through a honeymoon phase where they go full tilt at everything they wanted to do when they were working but couldn't due to time constraints and other obligations. While diving right into your new life is wonderful, it is important to pace yourself.

8. PLAN FOR UNKNOWNS.

You may not know what unknown expenditures will creep up on you in retirement, but know there will be some and create some flexibility for them in your budget.

I work with a couple who changed their retirement plan after learning that their two children, who are in their twenties, didn't have health insurance. They knew that if something happened, they wouldn't want to leave either of their kids in the hospital with unpaid bills. This knowledge and the fear that they might have to pay for their children's health care affected how they viewed their expenses in retirement as they cut back on some of their travel to create room in their budget for health insurance premiums.

Sometimes, unknowns will leave you with extra funds. For example, some people are frugal, so they end up having extra money at the end of every year. Others don't spend as aggressively as they thought they would, due to unforeseen circumstances. Some of my clients planned to provide for grandchildren who were never born, an unplanned circumstance that left more money in their pockets.

**THREE RETIREMENT INVESTMENT
PLANNING MISTAKES TO AVOID**

1. Markets change—don't take more investment risk than you can handle emotionally or financially.
2. Your retirement plan goes past your retirement date, so don't get too conservative too early.
3. Markets fall, but don't give up on your long-term investment plan. Keep a cash reserve to weather the storm.

Take a Closer Look at Your Career

Retirement doesn't have to mean that your career is over. It can be a gradual transition out of your career. It can also mean starting a new career part-time. If the idea of retiring "for good" gives you pause emotionally or financially, consider phasing out your career or starting an encore career.

PHASE IT OUT

Over the course of the last decade, more and more companies are offering the option of a phased retirement. In some scenarios, you can continue at your job on a part-time basis or as a freelancer. In other cases, you can mentor new recruits, providing valuable knowledge and expertise to those beginning their careers. There are several benefits to these types of arrangements: You stay socially engaged, your mind stays more acute and alert, and you have plenty of free time to explore other opportunities. Having some additional income doesn't hurt, either.

GO FOR THE ENCORE

Encore careers, or "second acts," have provided many retirees with high job satisfaction. In fact, new research shows that nine million Americans ages forty-four to seventy participate in encore careers.[48]

Many who have embarked on a new career during retirement have said that they had more satisfaction with their new career than with their previous career.[49] This makes sense because encores let you apply your human capital—the experiences and skills that you developed over the course of your life and career—to something new, something that might even be more aligned with your passions, creativity, and values.

You may be thinking, *Nope, I do not want to replace my job with another job. During the week, I want to wake up at nine o'clock, read the paper, head to exercise class, learn a new language, have time to plan and cook a healthy dinner, watch the evening news, and head to bed early. On the weekends, I want to spend time with my friends and family. I want to take a couple of vacations each year, and that's that.*

If this is you, bravo! You have a well-thought-out plan for how you want to spend your time in retirement. Not everyone needs to start a small business, become a community organizer, or volunteer at the local animal shelter. There should be no expectation to get out there and "do" just because you have the time.

The fact of the matter is that there is no one-size-fits-all solution to retirement. There is no rule book or a manual. Retirement can take many forms, and what is right for one person is not necessarily right for another. There are many different ways that you can be successful in retirement. Considering how you define success and

---

48   Miriam Salpeter, "Research Shows 9 Million Americans, Ages 44–70, now in 'Encore' Careers," press release, Keppie Careers, blog, https://www.keppiecareers.com/research-shows-9-million-americans-ages-44-70-now-in-encore-careers/.

49   Encore, "Encore Careers: The Persistence of Purpose," 2014, https://encore.org/wp-content/uploads/files/2014EncoreResearchOverview.pdf.

happiness is an important first step to identifying your retirement goals and plans. Take your time, don't pressure yourself, and see how your days will develop before you take on too much in retirement. Some retirees find themselves saying yes to all the new opportunities and quickly realize they are even busier than they were before retirement. It is important to maintain a mindful approach to your time in retirement.

ARE YOU READY FOR AN ENCORE?

Ask yourself the following questions to determine if you're ready for an encore.

- Am I financially ready to retire?

- Am I emotionally ready to retire?

- How will I spend my time? What other interests do I have?

- What would an ideal day in retirement look like? (This must be realistic. You cannot play golf or travel all day every day for the next twenty-plus years.)

When is Retirement Appropriate for You?

Retirement can be fraught with uncertainty, given the fact that many people will face a long retirement period of thirty years or more. While many factors need to come together to make a cohesive and sustainable long-term plan, the biggest concern most people face is the fear of making financial decisions based on emotion. Here are some ideas for decreasing anxiety and increasing clarity on the road to sound retirement planning.

Think Long-Term

Although many people plan for retirement with aspirations to live a certain lifestyle, they rarely understand that retirement takes place in phases.

The early years of retirement are often an opportunity to pursue activities that might not have been an option during your working years, such as traveling. Retirees are often still in good health, excited about their new lifestyle, and ready to do the things that they missed out on while they were working. For this reason, this phase is usually more expensive than the other phases, and can frequently be more expensive than your existing lifestyle.

The pace of the second phase of retirement is more leisurely. People start slowing down, traveling a bit less, and considering lifestyle options that are closer to home such as spending time with their children or grandchildren. Expenses tend to decrease during this phase.

In the third phase, many retirees will see their health care costs increase or need additional resources to stay in their home.

Failing to plan and save for all three phases can derail your retirement plan. A long retirement timeframe means being prepared for the entire twenty-five plus years ahead of you.

CONSIDER LIFESTYLE, HEALTH, AND FAMILY LONGEVITY

In addition to looking at your current lifestyle and health, look at your family's longevity. Do you have several centurions in your family, or do life expectancies dip slightly below the national average? Rather than looking at average life expectancies, family history can be a much better indicator of how long each of us can realistically expect to live. Having a realistic gauge of your longevity will help you make a long-term retirement plan. However, even if most everyone in your family lives well into their eighties, it's good to ask what happens if you become seriously ill five years into your retirement. What resources will you have to pay for the illness and sustain the rest of your retirement?

Identify Family Influence

Most people plan for retirement with an emphasis on their personal goals, or the goals they share with a significant other. However, it's also helpful to identify potential family commitments that might affect your retirement plan.

A long-term plan for retirement may include a family gifting component for the next generation, but it may also need to include contingency plans for situations in which your children or grandchildren need immediate financial assistance. We have worked with a number of clients who have had to help keep their kids' family afloat or cover medical or living expenses for family members. It's important to consider these possibilities, as they may require you to plan for contingencies to cover additional expenses.

Get Started Early

Early retirement planning gives you more options and opportunities to control the terms of your retirement than waiting to make a plan. It is the best way to improve your chances of accomplishing retirement goals. Even with advance planning, however, it can still be hard to turn off the final paycheck and begin living off your portfolio. Building a retirement plan many years before retirement occurs creates more flexibility over time to incorporate unexpected needs or expenses into that plan.

Empower Yourself

It's fairly common to have a myriad of retirement accounts with overlapping objectives, such as IRAs, 401(k)s, insurance policies, bank accounts, and other investments. Since most people are simply too busy working and saving to keep all of these accounts organized effectively, empowering yourself through financial organization helps to create a structure for your planning process.

Another opportunity to empower yourself in preparation for retirement is to schedule routine financial tune-ups. Similar to keeping your car in good shape, scheduling financial tune-ups creates time to check on your savings and spending goals so you stay on track with your retirement goals. This is a great time to reflect on potential life changes over the past year (family, work, lifestyle) that may have created opportunities to accelerate your retirement timeline, or potentially delay your retirement. Review your portfolio to make sure it still aligns with your retirement time frame and, possibly, rebalance investments to your targets if that can be done without creating a significant tax burden.

For many, trusting in a retirement plan that they proactively created to resolve any challenging issues in retirement is a source of comfort. Retirement planning can bring up a range of feelings, and knowing that they have diligently planned for a variety of contingencies can help even the most nervous people feel better.

How Do You Plan for Retirement as a Couple?

Planning for retirement as a couple brings unique challenges that single individuals will not face—namely, compromise and agreement.

For a couple to successfully enjoy their retirement together, they need to get the timing right, agree on a lifestyle, and decide how they will spend their time together.

TIME YOUR RETIREMENT

Married couples who have built a plan to retire simultaneously generally experience less stress and disagreement in retirement than those who have not. A dual retirement may reflect open lines of communication that helped the couple effectively prepare for retirement both financially and emotionally. In some cases, however, it is not possible for the couple to retire at the same time, which can strain the relationship.

The spouses may have worked together and developed a plan to retire at different times for a financial benefit. For example, having one spouse stay in the workforce can provide increased financial flexibility with ongoing cash flow and health benefits. There can also be a personal life benefit in allowing one spouse to establish a retirement identity with open lines of communication. One spouse may envision a lifestyle that includes travel, while the other spouse is not interested in traveling. This couple might work together so one spouse can retire early and plan adventure travel with friends while establishing a retirement identity.

When personal identity doesn't align with individual roles in the couple's relationship, retirement can cause tension. Some people may feel jealousy toward a spouse who continues to have a vibrant work life, while others may resent a spouse who is living a perceived life of leisure. In addition, failure to having clarity on household responsibilities can create conflict. A couple should have a shared understanding of how daily tasks such as cooking and cleaning may change or stay the same. A more successful approach to these situations is for the couple to maintain open lines of communication and help each other phase into new roles.

Couples also feel strain when one struggles to adjust to non-work life. People who were very connected at work and who were used to attending individual or group networking events might struggle to adjust when they no longer have a schedule filled with breakfast, coffee, and lunch meetings. People who had a professional leadership role may struggle when they are no longer in a position to give orders or when they try to treat their spouse as they would an employee.

DECIDE HOW TO SPEND TIME TOGETHER

It's never too early to start building and sharing your vision of retirement with your spouse. Couples run into conflict when they have different visions of what life in retirement will be like, where they will live, which activities or organizations they will be involved with, and if travel will be a significant part of their lives.

Talk about the issue of lifestyle and time with your spouse and then do a trial run. If you are accustomed to only spending nights and weekends together, then try spending every waking moment with each other. If that's too taxing, think about other ways to fill time away from each other during retirement. Find activities throughout the week that you enjoy doing separately and then make plans for what you'll do together in the evenings and on weekends.

A well-planned retirement that considers the financial and emotional impact of a major lifestyle shift can lead to a fulfilling, exciting next stage of life experience. But, as with any transition, how your retirement goes depends on the conversations you have and the actions you take before you reach retirement age.

Conversation Starters

1. What do you want your lifestyle to look like in retirement?

2. How will this lifestyle and the expenses associated with it change throughout the three phases of retirement?

3. How will you spend each of the forty hours you previously spent at work during retirement?

4. What do you want your retirement identity to look like?

5. What family obligations might affect your retirement?

6. How will you spend time together and apart?

7. Do you prefer to focus on leaving a legacy or taking "SKI Trips" ("SKI" meaning "Spending Kids' Inheritance")?

PART 3

Big
Conversations

F amily conversations regarding money, estate planning, retirement planning, elder care, and what will happen to investments when someone dies are not easy. However, these discussions are paramount to ensuring that a family's wealth is protected before a transfer takes place.

I encourage all of my clients to *talk* to their family about the financial, health, and lifestyle decisions they plan to make going into retirement.

Specifically, "*TALK*" is a guideline for framing family financial conversations:

- **T**alk about family financial discussions long before they are critical.
- **A**sk as many questions as you can think of no matter how tiny.
- **L**isten to each other with an understanding of one another's wants, needs, and emotions.
- **K**eep it up by continuing the conversation so you're constantly addressing new issues.

During most holidays and special family dinners, my family pulls out conversation starter cards that we keep in our dining room. These cards are great and lead to some really important conversations. They get us to *talk*, better understand each other's values, and connect with one another. The idea is that, by talking, we'll deepen our connections with one another by starting a conversation. We do the same for our clients at Flourish. We act as a facilitator for the hard money conversations everybody must have with their parents, kids, and their friends. In part 3 of this book, I'll explain why and how to have these conversations with the people that have the greatest impact on your life. I'll also show how these conversations have affected my clients and their personal money decisions.

CHAPTER 7

Even the Birds and the Bees Know Money Doesn't Grow on Trees— Talking to Your Kids about Finances

Talk to Your Kids

Before I started Flourish Wealth Management, my oldest daughter, Maddy, had a generous monthly allowance to cover all of her expenses including her clothes, car, haircuts, school lunches, personal care products, and more. Basically, we figured out what we were spending on Maddy and shifted the expenses to her so that she could learn how to budget and be responsible for spending decisions. I thought Jay and I were teaching her to budget, but when I started Flourish and told Maddy we were going to have to cut back on her allowance, she said, "I can't believe you are doing this to me." That's when I realized that, somewhere, I'd gone wrong. Maddy seemed overly focused on how the change in our financial situation would impact her personal spending. I was surprised, because Maddy had followed the spending and savings habits that Jay and I had set for her. She was a hard worker and started babysitting and working in retail as soon as possible to earn money and create a sense of financial independence. In junior high, she had a debit card and her own budget. When she was sixteen, she paid $3,000 that she had saved toward a used car. She'd always contributed and understood the value of a dollar, but something was different in her reaction. That's when I realized that we weren't making a conscious, daily effort to teach her about financial wants versus needs, and the value of sacrificing for a greater goal, such as starting Flourish.

Kids learn about their spending and savings habits from their parents. How they spend money begins with us. The challenge, however, is that 69 percent of parents are reluctant to discuss money with their kids.[50] In addition, 61 percent will only discuss money if their kids specifically ask about it. Unfortunately, finance is not a top priority of our education system. Fewer than 20 percent of teachers report feeling competent to teach personal finance and only seventeen states require high school students to take a personal finance course.[51] This means that the majority of your kids' financial education will come from you. You are teaching your kids whether you know it or not. Remember those early money memories that you experienced through your parents.

In Maddy's case, it wasn't that we weren't talking about money; it was that we weren't showing her our values concerning money on

---

50   T. Rowe Price, "Parents Are Likely to Pass Down Good and Bad Financial Habits to Their Kids," press release, (based on T. Rowe Price, *Parents, Kids & Money Survey*, 2017), (March 23, 2017): https://www.prnewswire.com/news-releases/t-rowe-price-parents-are-likely-to-pass-down-good-and-bad-financial-habits-to-their-kids-300428414.html.

51   Council for Economic Education, 2016 Survey of the States: National State of Financial & Economic Education, report, http://surveyofthestates.com/#challenge-0; Council for Economic Education, *2018 Survey of the States: Economic and Personal Finance Education in Our Nation's Schools*, report, http://councilforeconed.org/policy-and-advocacy/survey-of-the-states/.

a daily basis. Because we parents have such a great influence on how our kids spend, save, and invest, it's critical that we teach them early and often how we want them to value money. Starting Flourish was an important aspiration that aligned with our values and long-term goals despite some short-term financial sacrifices.

Teach Your Kids about Finance Early and Often

Parents have a unique opportunity to exhibit healthy behaviors for their children at all stages of their development. This partly requires talking about money, but it also requires using your actions to demonstrate how to manage it.

Every day brings natural learning opportunities for parents to introduce and explain financial concepts to their kids. Take advantage of these opportunities because they may not come again. In my family, we pull out conversation starter cards around the holidays or during family gatherings. The questions on these cards encourage our kids to think about their values related to numerous topics, including money. Recently, one card inspired our youngest, Grace, who is twelve, to begin thinking about our household bills. We asked her what kind of bills she thinks we might have, how we heat the house, and what else we might have to pay for just to keep things going. We also asked her how a mortgage works. While we didn't expect her to necessarily know the answer, it prompted her to think about the fixed expenses that it takes to run a household.

There are dozens of ways to start conversations with your kids about money. How you start them is less important than getting them started. Below are some lessons and conversations that can help your kids learn about finance during each developmental stage.

GRADE SCHOOL

Grade school offers opportunities for basic conversations about saving, investing, income, and spending.

- Have conversations about needs versus wants.

- Talk, as a family, about what you are saving for, such as an upcoming vacation or a house project.

- Talk about charities that you support in terms of dollars and time.

- Teach your kids how to give back by having them donate toys or items that they no longer use.

- Use cash for some purchases to teach your kids how to count and use money.

- Show how to comparison-shop, whether it is at the store or online, while discussing pros and cons relative to the price of the product.

- Discuss how getting an education can affect future earning power.

- Use an allowance to introduce the three primary purposes of money: saving, sharing, and spending.

- Consider a piggy bank (physical or virtual) that has three slots to separate dollars for saving, sharing, and spending. You can pick the ratio between the slots. For example, one-third of the total dollars could go to each category, or it could be a ratio that aligns with your family values.

- Introduce the experience of delayed gratification by helping your child set a saving goal for a future item.

- Discuss the reasons why and when someone might want to borrow money.

- Teach the basics of investing for the future in stocks and bonds, along with the concept of risk and reward. Keep it simple and use real-life examples. Talk about your kids' favorite products and relate this back to the companies that make the products. Describe how a stock is an opportunity to own a small part of that company and that the value can go up and down, but over the long term, you hope the company will be more valuable. Explain that, with a bond, you are lending money that will get repaid in the future, but in the meantime you will receive interest.

Allowances are a great way to teach grade school kids about spending and saving. There is some debate here, but I prefer setting an allowance that is not tied to the daily chores that are expected of each family member. Allowances can be a powerful tool to teach money management skills such as budgeting and saving. Additional earning opportunities can be tied to occasional one-time jobs or projects such as cleaning out the garage or kitchen cabinets. I recommend avoiding letting your kids have advances on their allowance so they can buy something that costs more than they have saved. Although many parents are happy to advance a loan, they rarely have the discipline to demand repayment, much less charge interest.

It's important to teach grade school kids about money in a tangible way. While they can't understand how a plastic card can buy groceries or pay bills, they will understand the connection between the money in their piggy bank and the new toy they've bought. Giving young kids a physical foundation regarding how money works and then introducing them to the concept of credit is helpful.

MIDDLE SCHOOL

In middle school, children are capable of understanding finance on a deeper level. As a parent, you should take the concepts they learned in grade school and expand upon them. Some possible discussion areas include the following:

- Review the importance of daily budgets, including how and why they are created, along with tools to support staying on budget.

- Revisit the topic of allowances to continue the theme of share, save, and spend. Revisit the appropriate amount for each category.

- Continue conversations about charitable giving. Consider a family pool for charitable dollars where each family member can have a vote or nominate a charity.

- Consider a matching program for saving or sharing opportunities. For example, for every dollar your child saves or gives away to charity, match it by 50 percent or a formula that feels comfortable to you.

- Encourage them to save to reinforce the benefits of delayed gratification. This is an important age for kids to realize how their financial decisions impact long-term and short-term goals (e.g., if they buy that candy now, they are going to have to work longer to pay for the video game they really want).

- Talk about advertising and peer pressure for fad items.

- Create a one-time budget for back-to-school shopping, and work with them on getting ready for school.

- Get kids involved in spending decisions, including big-ticket items such as a new or used car, plus the complicated considerations that go into this purchase.

- Bring kids to a bank or credit union to open a savings account.

- Introduce the types of insurance coverage and the purpose for insurance.

- Discuss the importance of protecting one's identity online by never sharing personal or credit information.

- Discuss inflation and why items cost more each year.

- Explain credit cards and how they work, along with the importance of paying the monthly balance each month.

- Introduce the concept of compound interest and the power it has on long-term savings; there are many online tools to illustrate this concept including that of the US Securities and Exchange Commission: https://www.investor.gov/ additional-resources/free-financial-planning-tools/ compound-interest-calculator.

- Don't put all your eggs in one basket. Diversification is important in an investment plan. Discuss various ways to invest money, including stocks, bonds, real estate, and other noncash assets.

- Introduce college savings with information on any savings that are in place already, plans to save for the future, along with your own and your spouse's college experience.

Adolescence is a good time for kids to practice the financial skills they've learned from you because it's one of few times in their lives when they can make mistakes that will not affect their life in a major way. Give them a set amount of spending money for a vacation or a family outing and make them stick to it. This teaches responsibilities and, sometimes, consequences.

A "Valuable" Lesson

One client told me that when he was young his family went on vacation each year, and each year each kid got $25 to spend while on vacation. The first year, he spent all of his allowance on the first day. He cried and begged his parents for more money as he watched his siblings spend money on the things they wanted throughout the trip, but his parents didn't cave. He didn't make the same mistake the following year. This little exercise teaches children to make decisions, prioritize, and depend on themselves. If you give them more money when they overspend, you ruin the lesson.

HIGH SCHOOL

Ideally, high school prepares students for college, the working world, and for taking on adult responsibilities. But as I mentioned before, most high schools are not teaching students about finance so the responsibility falls to parents, who can teach high school students in the following ways.

- You can get your teens their first debit card to learn how to manage funds and deal with overdraft consequences.

- Have your teens track spending to maintain a budget via an app, such as Mint.

- You can consider shifting the responsibility for paying for more of their daily expenses via an increased allowance.

- Revisit the bucketing conversation to ensure they maintain a save, share, spend approach within the budgeting process.

- Explain the financial implications of college, not only what it costs but also how student loans and grants work, and the additional financial opportunities your kids will have if they earn a degree.

- You can share more details about their college savings plan and how it works. You can also use this conversation as an opportunity to share your goals or the expectations you have for funding their college education. This could include expectations for your child's contribution or thoughts on student loans.

- You can instruct your teens about how to prepare for adult responsibilities such as saving for a car and/or a house, and saving for retirement.

- You can explain how to compare credit cards and the benefits and drawbacks they offer and how to manage credit cards in a way that avoids interest accrual.

- You can teach your teens what credit scores are and why they matter.

- You can describe the different types of insurance offered, why they matter, and how things such as copayments and deductibles work.

- You can encourage a part-time job for income and the opportunity for some financial independence. If this isn't possible during the school year, you can ask the teens to consider a summer job.

- You can help your teens understand what taxes are taken out of their paychecks and why this occurs.

- You can help your teens set up their first investment account, such as a Roth IRA, when they have earnings.

- You can encourage your teens to build a savings account for out-of-the ordinary expenses or opportunities that may come up, and the importance of keeping a cash reserve

- Explain the Rule of 72, which is how long it takes to double your money (divide seventy-two by your estimated rate of return and the result is how long it will take to double your money, so an investment earning 6 percent a year will double in twelve years).

WANTS VERSUS NEEDS

Every conversation you have with your children about finances, regardless of their age, is a great opportunity to segue into a discussion about wants versus needs. Asking kids whether they want or need something before they make a purchase really gets them thinking about their own money values.

Use Pop Culture and Technology to Your Advantage

Pop culture is a phenomenal resource for teaching kids about finance. When Maddy was four, she told me that we should help people who are homeless. She told me this while we were driving, and I remember thinking how great it was that Maddy was thinking about homeless people.

When we got home, I asked Maddy what got her thinking about helping homeless people. She said, "Well, I was watching SpongeBob SquarePants and Squidward was homeless and had to live in a box. It's not good to live in a box in the water, because it disintegrates."

So while I thought I had helped Maddy understand how to help others, SpongeBob and the disintegrating box had actually done the work. While pop culture got one of my kids thinking about giving back, it got another thinking about investing.

Not long ago, Fernando, my most financially carefree child, asked me to invest in a stock on his behalf. I was pleasantly surprised but knew that I'd have to find a relatable way to teach him about investing to keep him interested. I got on Stockpile, a kid-friendly app that allows users to buy partial shares and that gives interesting, easy to understand backgrounds about each company. Using Stockpile led to conversations about what kinds of products and companies my twelve-year-old son might relate to, which led him to investing in Apple. We ended up matching Fernando's $60 investment so he had $120 to invest. Almost immediately, the stock dropped, which was great because it taught Fernando what can happen in the market. Since then, the stock has gone up.

As a family, we use Kiva.org to make small loans to people in Guatemala, which is where Fernando and Grace were born. The opportunity to incorporate another culture into our family has been an important theme of adoption, with the benefit of using this technology to introduce the power of money at an early age. It's a rewarding conversation when a relatively small amount of money can make a significant impact in a county like Guatemala, particularly when your kids can identify with the value of investing in supplies for a food co-op or a weaving guild to support a small business.

Using tools such as Stockpile and Kiva is just another way we can use technology to create money experiences for our kids. Regardless of which money lesson you're teaching your children, pop culture and technology can be powerful tools for driving home financial lessons when used effectively.

Honor Their Differences

Even though Jay and I are raising each of our three children with the same financial values, we have to remember that they're individuals and, while we have influenced some of their financial values, they still have their own approaches to money.

Maddy's attitude to finance has changed a lot from the entitled days when we talked to her about reducing her budget before we started Flourish. Today, she's quite frugal. She's a hard worker and a saver, and she funds a Roth contribution with her own money each year.

Fernando is impulsive. When he has money or a gift card, he spends it. He can't even wait for Amazon to deliver something; he'd rather go to Target for immediate gratification. He also isn't that motivated to save or work for extra money, although his interest in the stock market has given me hope that his values might change.

Grace, who is also twelve, is a hard worker, as Maddy is. She always has a stash of money, but she never wants to spend it. Grace is the person who can carry a mini purse with $40 through a mall all day without spending a dime and then lends her brother $20 that he probably won't pay back because he sees something he "absolutely needs right now."

Even if you teach your kids the same money values, it's important to understand that they will each bring their own personal style to spending, saving, and investing.

Have Conversations about Debt and Earning

With 67 percent of millennials spending more than they earn and the average American having $15,654 in credit card debt, teaching kids about earning and debt is critical to their financial future.[52]

Fernando got a real-life lesson in earning and debt when he was nine. As I mentioned, unlike my girls, Fernando has a hard time not spending money. When he was nine, we got him the *Clash of Clans* video game. It had an online community playing option that we didn't sign up for because we knew we couldn't police Fernando's interactions. Well, I'd recently gotten a new credit card and Fernando got ahold of it. He entered the number and signed up for the online subscription with a fake e-mail address. It took Jay and me forever to get the subscription canceled because it didn't link to our e-mail addresses, obviously. When Fernando and I had the conversation about how he didn't have permission to spend my money, he said, "Well, that's not money. That's just a credit card." So even though it was a less than ideal situation, it opened the door for a lesson about credit cards and how they work, and it was a much more effective conversation than it would have been without the experience of the *Clash of Clans* subscription.

When Maddy was a freshman in college, we opened a credit card for her so she could understand how it worked while also building credit that she would need for a future car or home loan. After a few months, I realized that Maddy had never used her card. When I asked why, she said, "I don't want to miss the monthly payment because then I'll ruin my credit."

That opened the door for me to explain that she had to use the card to *establish* credit. To eliminate Maddy's fears about making a late payment, we set up an automatic withdrawal from her checking account to make her credit card payments. These are just two examples of how parents can use daily situations and conversations to help prepare their kids for financial success.

---

52 Erin El Issa, "2017 American Household Credit Card Debt Study," NerdWallet, https://www.nerdwallet.com/blog/average-credit-card-debt-household/.

Teach Them How to Earn

These days, many families can afford to buy more for their children than their parents were able to buy for them. However, teaching your kids to earn has tremendous value. If your child wants to go to an expensive summer camp, set a reasonable amount that your child can earn toward the camp. Help your child think of ways to earn the money. This might include doing extra chores, babysitting, walking the neighbor's dog, raking yards, mowing lawns, washing cars, or helping a senior with basic house cleaning. Not only does this teach kids how to earn, it also increases their confidence that they can earn and complete tasks and achieve goals.

All parents want their kids to grow up to be happy adults, yet most parents don't realize how critical it is to teach their kids about healthy financial habits and values. Helping your children develop healthy money habits today will increase their chances for a happier life.

CLIENT STORY
How One Millennial Learned about Finance

We worked with a millennial team member looking to make her first home purchase. Unfortunately she ran into numerous complications from money decisions that were made before and during college. In retrospect, she would have made different financial decisions over the prior ten years if she had known the long-term implications. Her situation is very common these days as millennials find that their college decisions and debt burdens directly affect opportunities to qualify for a home mortgage, make car payments, manage expenses, and address personal debt. She was frustrated to look back on uninformed decisions made simply because she never had conversations with her parents about how her spending decisions might limit long-term planning opportunities.

Using this example, we encourage parents to introduce budgeting concepts as early as possible. Parents constantly give kids advice to help them stay out of trouble, but they don't always provide detailed money advice. Although some parents initiate conversations about money, they don't include in-depth education about budgeting. Most teens don't naturally know how to manage expenses, balance a checkbook, or establish spending limits. It is important for parents to take the lead on introducing concepts about short- and long-term goals so kids can have a framework for making their own decisions.

Another important money conversation parents should initiate is the importance of setting money goals. Balancing short-term and long-term goals is not intuitive to most people, because short-term spending can eliminate the opportunity to pursue a wide variety of unforeseen long-term goals. For example, our millennial team member and her husband saved money to pay for their dream wedding (an amazing, one-day experience) without knowing that it might have been a better decision to apply those dollars toward a house down payment (a lifetime of family memories). Although they loved the wedding day, they would have reconsidered the total amount budgeted for the wedding relative to their future goals. Parents can have a conversation with their kids about how much money has been saved for college, weddings, and other big expenses to support their making more effective financial decisions. It would also be helpful to have conversations about potential long-term career goals to understand if postgraduate education is necessary so those expenses can be factored into college budgeting decisions. Teaching kids about the expenses they will face in the real world provides a better context for short-term budgeting decisions during and after college.

Finally, our millennial team member always wished that somebody had told her the impact debt would have on a home purchase. Many millennials have started careers and earn a decent living, but they haven't been able to save the amount needed to create financial flexibility long-term. In this case, the home mortgage prequalification process was a crash course in how debt placed significant limitations on the house they could buy. Our team member and her husband both easily identified multiple financing decisions that they would have changed if somebody had clearly explained the long-term implications.

Talking about financial decisions with your kids will help them feel more comfortable with money and provide a foundation for making future decisions on their own. Although our team member didn't have enough context to understand that her short-term financial decisions would have such a huge impact on her opportunities after college, particularly when working to purchase a home, her experience, hopefully, can provide a better roadmap for other families.

Actions Speak Louder than Words

Our kids learn from what we do or don't do more than anything we tell them. Do they see you donate time or money to charities? Do you talk about saving for a family vacation or other big-ticket items? Do they see you research for the best price/value on an item that you are looking to purchase, or do you buy the first one you see? Do you explain how you choose between similar products at the grocery store? Is it based on quality, or price per unit? Kids not only learn how to make financial decisions from their parents but also tend to follow in their parents' footsteps. Just look at these statistics:

Parents' Savings Influences Kids' Future Savings

Parents who have at least three types of savings (e.g., retirement savings, emergency fund, college savings, or money saved for another goal) have kids who are more likely to save (98 percent) than parents who do not have three types of savings (86 percent).[53]

Bankruptcy Affects Kids

 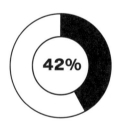

The kids of parents who have declared bankruptcy usually spend money as soon as they get it (71 percent) versus kids of parents who have not declared bankruptcy (42 percent).[54]

---

53 T. Rowe Price, "Parents Are Likely to Pass Down Good and Bad Financial Habits to Their Kids," press release, Mar. 23, 2017, (based on T. Rowe Price, *Parents, Kids & Money Survey*, 2017), https://www.prnewswire.com/news-releases/t-rowe-price-parents-are-likely-to-pass-down-good-and-bad-financial-habits-to-their-kids-300428414.html.

54 Ibid.

One of my clients always said yes to her daughter, who was struggling to get on her feet. As a result, the daughter's spending was out of line. This client eventually realized that she wasn't really helping her daughter and ended up developing a plan to get her daughter to take more responsibility for her finances. It was a tough but necessary conversation. With some career decisions and lifestyle changes, the daughter is now living within her means and making good financial choices.

While educating your children about how to manage money is important, you have to practice what you preach. Think about the messages your spending, saving, and investing choices send to your kids.

Conversation Starters

1. How much do you think it costs to run this house and what monthly bills do we pay? Do you understand how a credit card works?

2. Can you think of a time we saved our money to buy something? How long did it take us to save enough money to buy it?

3. What is the difference between saving, spending, and sharing?

4. Why do we need to save money?

5. What is debt and how can debt affect the way we want to live our lives?

6. What is financial success?

7. What charitable causes would you like to support and why?

8. What is your earliest money memory?

9. How do you determine if an expense falls into the want versus need category?

CHAPTER 8

Senior Support— Discussing Late-Life Finances with Your Parents

Talk to Your Parents

About six years ago, my mom was diagnosed with stage four Hodgkin's lymphoma cancer. I was shocked by the diagnosis. Our immediate concern was to find the best medical care possible, meaning we had to move my mom and dad from their cabin life in Northern Wisconsin to Minneapolis, where she would have access to significantly better medical care. My parents lived with us during the six-month-long treatment period, which was both a blessing and a challenge. While the doctors were trying to treat my mom's cancer, Jay and I had to juggle work and family to drive her to medical appointments while keeping track of her treatment plan. At the same time, the shock of the cancer diagnosis took a big toll on my parents so we needed to give them extra emotional support. This also turned our house upside down, as we had to make space for my parents, so we moved Grace and Fernando into the same bedroom together, adding bunkbeds and updating bathrooms along the way. It was one of the most chaotic times of my life.

I am happy to say that my mom has been cancer-free for over five years. However, the medical crisis her cancer caused made me realize the importance of getting in front of medical and financial matters before it's too late.

Because of my career choice, I was knowledgeable about my parents' finances. I had helped them with long-term care insurance, life insurance policies, and investment choices, so fortunately my parents' finances were in order before my mom got sick and they had the right resources to financially sustain the treatment plan. However, in most families, the kids struggle to sort through and manage their finances when a parent becomes ill. This happens because most families don't talk about finance, insurance, long-term care, and estate planning until someone gets sick.

More than fifteen years ago, Jay's father had a stroke, a life-threatening event. Jay was prompted to discuss finances with his mom as they evaluated life options in the event that his father wasn't able to leave the hospital. At the time, Jay's dad was a senior partner at a large law firm. Jay's mom didn't work outside the home and she wasn't involved with managing the finances. After talking to her, Jay quickly realized she would have no idea how to manage their financial affairs if Jay's dad died. Jay and his brothers weren't much help; they'd never discussed finances with their parents. Of course, this all changed once Jay's dad had a stroke. He ended up recovering, fortunately, but the family could have faced some real challenges sorting out the finances had things turned out differently. More recently, each of the boys met with their dad to share the details of their parents' finances and estate plan.

Not knowing your parents' financial situation and their plans for health care, insurance, and living puts you and your family at a financial risk. The costs associated with caring for a parent who doesn't have enough resources, the right health care options, housing situation, or the right savings and investment plan can place a tremendous financial burden on the kids. If the parents do not have the financial resources or an effective medical plan in place, it can affect how much the children can work during an extended medical situation, how much they can save, and how much they can invest. Yet, most of the time, we wait until there is a crisis to talk about finances with our parents.

CARING FOR YOUR PARENTS BY THE NUMBERS[55]

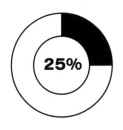 **25%**

Twenty-five percent of baby boomers are caring for an aging parent.

Two out of three caregivers are women.

 **$350,000**

Lost wages and Social Security benefits for those caring for aging parents average $350,000 a person.

---

55 Fidelity Investments, "How to Take Care of Aging Parents and Yourself," Fidelity Viewpoints, Sept. 27, 2017, https://www.fidelity.com/viewpoints/personal-finance/caring-for-aging-parents.

When I work with clients, I always ask about their parents' health and finances. More often than not they have no idea how their parents are positioned financially or what will happen when their parents die. Although talking about long-term financial and health care plans may be uncomfortable, it is important to initiate conversations about these important topics with your parents before a medical emergency or financial crisis arrives. Below are eight questions that will help you better understand what your parents need and what they want to happen when they pass.

1. DO YOU HAVE KEY DOCUMENTS IN PLACE?

Key documents include wills, durable power of attorney, and health care directives. You need to know if these documents exist, where they are stored, and when they were last updated. You also need to know who your parents have appointed to act on their behalf if something happens and they're no longer capable of making their own financial decisions.

2. WHEN WAS THE LAST TIME YOU REVIEWED THE BENEFICIARIES OF YOUR RETIREMENT AND INSURANCE ASSETS?

Many people update their wills without updating the beneficiaries on their retirement and insurance policies. This is a crucial misstep that can result in the wrong person benefiting from their assets because beneficiary information always overrules what is stated in the will.

3. HAVE YOU CREATED A LIST INDICATING HOW YOUR PERSONAL ITEMS SHOULD BE DIVIDED?

Personal property, such as family jewelry, china, or heirlooms, can be a huge source of family conflict. To avoid disputes, include in your plan how these items should be divided amongst children. It can be surprising what leads to tension, because the item in question may not be costly but hold sentimental value. I suggest that clients talk to kids ahead of time to gauge their interest on items meaningful to them and then complete a written property distribution list as part of their estate plan. This is simply a signed, written document listing the items and who receives each one. It can be updated at any time. The list can be an informal, simple, handwritten letter that details which items will be gifted and who will receive them. A little planning can prevent hard feelings among siblings and ensure that everyone gets what they want.

CLIENT STORY
Cabin Conflict

In our home state of Minnesota it's common for people to have a second home on a lake. Interestingly, these homes can cause a lot of conflict when the owners die. For example, a client inherited a cabin with her brother. The brother didn't want to use the cabin, but he also didn't want to sell his half to my client. Instead, he let his kids use the cabin, which caused problems for my client. Suddenly, instead of having this serene place to relax, she had to share it with nieces and nephews who didn't treat it with the same level of respect that she did. In another situation, one of my clients couldn't afford to buy his other siblings out of a cabin that only he wanted to keep. As a result, he had to sell the cabin even though the parents' desire was to keep the cabin in the family. The parents could have avoided the situation if they'd had a conversation ahead of time or, potentially, could have set up a fund to help pay for the cabin's upkeep before they passed. Having conversations about property is particularly important when it involves real estate, which comes with other potential complications.

4. WHO ARE YOUR KEY ADVISORS?

Typically, your parents' list of key advisors will include a financial planner, attorney, accountant, and insurance agents. Get to know these people and invite them to a joint meeting so you know exactly what is happening with your parents' finances and long-term care. At Flourish, we often host family meetings where we include the parents, grown children, and any other trusted advisor. While these meetings don't always include detailed financial numbers (based on the clients' preferences), they provide an important sense of comfort regarding the overall state of the parents' finances and create the foundation for future conversations.

Some families also choose to work with an elder care coordinator. Elder care coordinators will help manage the medical and home decisions for your parents. They can be a great outside, neutral source of help to facilitate productive conversations with your parents.

5. HAVE YOU CREATED A LETTER OF LAST INSTRUCTIONS?

A letter of last instructions isn't a legal document, but it will include helpful information to identify your parents' financial information and wishes for the future. A letter of instruction will provide a detailed list of your parents' assets and liabilities, insurance policies, key advisors, credit card numbers, contact information for friends and family, location of all key documents such as birth certificates, Social Security cards, marriage papers, the location and keys of any safe deposit boxes, information about any burial plans, and wishes for their funeral. In our modern world, the letter of last instructions should also include a plan to share usernames and passwords to access key accounts and subscriptions.

It is a great practice to update this document annually and make sure that the appropriate people know where it is. One of my clients has all of this information in a big black binder. The family jokes about it, but the efforts he's put into organizing his documents will make things much easier for his family when he passes.

6. DO YOU HAVE ENOUGH RESOURCES TO COVER YOUR RETIREMENT, HOUSING, AND MEDICAL COSTS?

You should know how long your parents plan to stay in their home, what housing options are acceptable to them throughout the aging process, and whether they have resources available to afford those housing plans. While my parents didn't want to leave Wisconsin and returned to cabin living once my mom was better, they are starting to realize that they can't manage their house alone. Someday, they will have to permanently live closer to us so we can help care for them. During conversations about housing, also ask difficult questions about your parents' ability to pay for future medical care and long-term care policies.

It's also important to discuss details about who will take over paying the bills in the event that your parents no longer have the ability to keep on top of their day-to-day bills. There may also be logistical benefits to designating one person to pay all of the bills. For example, I take over paying my parents' bills when they vacation in Arizona every winter. It's easier and safer than having all of their documents transferred to Arizona and then back to the Midwest again in the summer.

7. WHO SHOULD BE NOTIFIED IF INSURANCE PAYMENTS ARE MISSED?

Key insurance policies should have a backup person who's notified if a payment isn't made. I heard a tragic story about an individual who lost insurance after years of paying for a long-term-care insurance policy because she missed her payment and the follow-up notices from the insurance company. Adding back-up contact information is a simple process using a form that can be filed with the insurance company.

8. WHAT ROLE WILL EACH SIBLING PLAY IN THE MANAGEMENT OF THE ASSETS?

Who manages what for your parents can be tricky. Sibling dynamics that existed in childhood will flare up almost immediately, particularly if these conversations take place *during* a crisis. To avoid this uncomfortable and unproductive situation, assemble the siblings and define the role of each if an unexpected illness or event occurs. That way, everyone knows which role they're expected to play. For instance, one sibling might agree to transport your parents to their doctor appointments; another might agree to manage their bills; and another might agree to help them sell their house and move them into a long-term living facility. Crisis preplanning prevents one sibling from feeling overwhelmed by the burden of caring for aging parents. Conversations with your siblings are really about coming together on a shared purpose: helping your parents. The key is to communicate, communicate, communicate.

Even if you're not the person managing your parents' finances, pay attention to odd spending behaviors. Watch for unexpected changes in their estate plan as that's often a sign that something isn't right. Approximately one in ten Americans aged sixty or older have endured some form of elder abuse by family members, particularly financial abuse.[56] Know who is caring for your parents, pay attention to who is spending time with them, and question unusual financial decisions.

One of my clients, Josephine, who was experiencing some challenges in making decisions, left her financial decisions to her son. At first, the son seemed super helpful, but then Josephine's spending started to increase, which made no sense because she had recently sold some real estate which should have lowered her spending. We asked if we could start looking through her bank statements. That's when we noticed that she was paying for a BMW that we knew she didn't have. We ended up going to her house and suggested she talk to her other kids about what was happening. She was surprised and reluctant to confront her son, who did have a BMW. Eventually, she agreed to get the other children involved to work through this challenge.

Handling In-Laws

Sometimes, parents prefer to have financial meetings that include immediate family only, so no in-laws. They don't want their kids bringing their spouses because they don't want the spouses to know

---

56   National Council on Aging (NCOA), "Elder Abuse Facts," https://www.ncoa.org/ public-policy-action/elder-justice/elder-abuse-facts/.

too much about their financial situation. In some ways, this is silly because most people will go straight home and tell their spouses about the conversation anyway. However, prepare for this option and decide if excluding in-laws from the family meeting will help or hinder the conversation.

CLIENT STORY

Never Put All Your Eggs in One Basket, Especially if it's Loosely Woven

June, another client, also raised red flags for us at Flourish, as well as for her daughter, when she started taking investment advice from her brother. One day, June called and asked if she owned any S&P 500. She explained that all she wanted in her portfolio was Google and Facebook because "those stocks are only going up." I was curious about what prompted the change, so I asked her about it. She said her brother gave her this recommendation and she trusted his advice because he was wealthy and "really smart" when it came to investing. I told her about the potential downside of owning one type of investment, particularly risky investments such as technology stocks. She replied that her brother would never lose money and guaranteed the investment. After some discussion, I called June's daughter whom we had permission to speak with to share my concerns about this proposed investment plan. Her daughter shared that the brother with the investment advice was actually ninety-four years old and living in a nursing home. Today, with some intervention from both June's daughter and son, we were able to prevent June from making a drastic investment move.

Regardless of how open your family has been with conversations about money matters in the past, some of these eight questions may stretch beyond your personal comfort level. The important thing to focus on is creating a productive conversation. Being honest about the difficulty of raising these questions is a great start to form a common bond, which can be reaffirmed by reiterating that the conversation is designed to benefit your parents and support the achievement of their postretirement goals. The additional benefits will be experienced by future generations through a smooth transition of values, priorities, and assets.

Timing is Everything

Talking to parents about their finances, especially those who are reluctant to share financial information, can be an issue of timing. Avoid talking to them about finances during the holiday seasons as the added stress may not lead to a productive meeting. Instead, think about coordinating with your sibling(s) to determine who should lead the money conversation. Start with logistical questions and then lead to deeper questions about the health of their finances and medical plans. For example, ask about their retirement plans and then move on to more specific issues such as whether they have a will, financial power of attorney, and a health care directive. This approach will likely require multiple meetings, but they don't have to be formal. Gradually gather this information in a setting where your parents feel comfortable. In general, it is much easier to get organized when your parents are in good shape rather than when they are in the emergency room.

Many times, there's a general misconception that the only reason people ask their parents about money is for their own benefit. Ideally, the conversations you have with your parents about finance should be intended to find out if they have a good plan in place and what you and your siblings can do to help them.

Finances shouldn't drive every one of your life decisions, but everyone should be aware of how their parents' health, finance, and long-term care plans might affect their own well-being.

Conversation Starters

1. What are your parents' thoughts on long-term housing?

2. Do they have their key documents in place?

3. Who are the key advisors your parents rely on?

4. What's their vision for health care?

5. What role will your siblings play in managing your parents' finances and long-term health care?

6. Do they have the financial resources to support their spending?

7. What type of insurance do your parents have?

8. Who are they talking to about Medicare?

9. Do they need help getting government or pension benefits?

10. Have they made funeral arrangements?

CHAPTER 9

Friends and Finances *Do* Mix

Seventy percent of us think it's inappropriate and rude to talk about personal finance in a social setting, yet our friends are our some of our greatest influencers.[57] Friends influence how we act, how stressed we feel, how long we live, the choices we make, the risks we take, our self-control, and the way we manage our finances.[58] Yet, as recently as 2009, Miss Manners, one of the most popular lifestyle columnists, advised her readers not to talk about finances.[59]

Several years ago, I attended a training conference led by Elizabeth Jetton, a thought leader in the financial planning profession who is well known for gathering women financial advisors in

57 Ally Bank, "Holiday Tip: Most Americans Say Social Conversations about Money are Taboo, According to Ally Bank's Money Talks Study," press release, Nov. 24, 2015, https://media.ally.com/2015-11-24-Holiday-Tip-Most-Americans-Say-Social-Conversations-About-Money-are-Taboo-According-to-Ally-Banks-Money-Talks-Study.

58 Amy Morin, "5 Surprising Ways Your Friends Influence You, Backed by Science," *Huffington Post*, April 14, 2015 (updated June 14, 2015), https://www.huffington-post.com/amy-morin/friends-health-science_b_7042042.html.

59 Miss Manners, "Don't Discuss Money with Neighbors," Uexpress, Aug. 25, 2009, http://www.uexpress.com/miss-manners/2009/8/25/dont-discuss-money-with-neighbors.

a "circle" to talk about important issues. Money is a key topic to help women find their voice. The circle process is a way to empower and engage women in their communities to change the conversation about money. The intent of these gatherings it to create a foundation for helping women open up to new friends about finance and support meaningful conversations.

I had always wanted to attend one of Elizabeth's circle trainings because of the deep experience and openness that it offers. When I attended the circle, before we started talking about finance, Elizabeth laid out some protocols including having a talking stick: only the person holding it can speak. By preventing a free-for-all conversation, Elizabeth immediately facilitated a deeper, more meaningful conversation among participants. She stopped our need to constantly respond to people and, instead, encouraged us to sit back and reflect on the comments being made.

First, we started with easier opening conversations that had nothing to do with finance, such as:

- What do you want to add to your personal and professional life that is currently missing?

- What are the most important challenges you face in life?

- What brought you joy when you were younger?

- What would you need to let go of so you could have more time for the important things?

- Can you add something to your life as a theme, not as a task?

- Are you able to effectively summarize the most important values in your life?

This allowed for a reconnection with ourselves while also letting us get to know each other, building trust and conviction for deeper connections. Eventually, we moved into financial conversations that led with questions such as:

- Is money a plus or a minus in your daily life?

- Where do you invest your time, talent, and money?

- What money conversations should you be having in your life? What money conversations are you avoiding?

- What parts of your life should you invest in now to support your long-term goals?

- How do you know if your values are in line with your finances?

- Who would you most like to build a money connection with?

- Can you share your money story with friends and family?

The benefit of this type of exercise is that the conversations triggered deeper revelations about our personal values and what we needed to do to move through some of the blockages in our life. At the time, I was feeling resentment toward Jay because he believed he still had to be the main breadwinner after losing his job. I had to work through those feelings. I asked myself what was getting in the way of my working through those emotions, what I would be willing to let go of, and what might make Jay more open to the conversations I wanted to have. After the training, I went home and had a conversation with Jay that helped me gain some acceptance of a money situation that had been bothering me.

The other women in the circle helped me work through a money matter. I was able to work through an emotional piece of money management that was bothering me without sharing intimate financial details. Because our friends are so influential, they can help us break down money barriers, provide support, offer different perspectives about managing money, and encourage us to take more control of our finances.

Friends Help Us Break Down Barriers

Many barriers prevent us from initiating money conversations with our family. Family should be our closest ally, but when money and emotions get involved, we often find ourselves falling into old family roles, feeling resentment toward certain family members, or feeling awkward about bringing up important money discussions. With friends, we can often open up in a way that isn't possible with family. With friends, those barriers and roles don't exist.

When one of my girlfriends was going through a divorce, she opened up to me about the financial decisions that had been made before the divorce and that really affected her. It was a conversation she wouldn't have had with a family member, who might have had clouded her judgment about the situation or might have judged her decisions unfairly. I know that being able to talk with a trusted friend about those money decisions and her anxiety about them was really freeing for this friend.

Friends Provide Support

Sometimes, verbalizing our money goals with our friends can help us achieve them. Friends provide support and accountability in a way that we may not get or want to get from other people who influence our decisions. For example, if you want to learn more about giving to organizations or if you want to work with your spouse to set up an allowance structure for your kids, telling a friend about your plans will increase the chance that you'll follow through on them. Accountability is a very powerful tool that can be used to your advantage in situations like this. Your friends might also have some ideas to help you achieve your goals, which brings me to my next point.

Friends Offer Different Perspectives

Talking with friends, such as the women I met in the circle, offers a different perspective on how you might want to handle your own money decisions. All individuals and all families choose to approach and manage money differently. The only way to learn about your friends' best practices is to start talking to them about finance.

I get ideas from friends all the time. It was from a friend that I learned about creating parameters for each couple's spending limits, which I talked about in part 1 of this book. She mentioned that she and her husband put a $500 spending limit on purchases. They didn't have to tell each other about anything under that amount. I now recommend that my clients who are struggling to get on the same financial page as their spouse take the same approach.

A key thing to remember here is that the point of having money conversations with your friends isn't to become their financial advisor. It's much more focused on learning from each other and supporting each other.

> The point of having money conversations with your friends isn't to become their financial advisor.

Money conversations build a foundation for richer conversations in the future through shared vulnerability and authenticity.

Friends Encourage Us to Take Greater Interest in Our Finances

Many of us don't know the details of our finances because our partner takes the lead. Talking to friends indirectly encourages us to take more interest in something that affects every aspect of our lives. Mentioning something such as a 401(k) plan or how you approach your own investments might get your friends thinking about their own investments.

You don't need to get naked with your finances, but sharing general thoughts about goals and priorities can be helpful. The goal is to learn, be curious, connect more to your money values, be better prepared for a conversation that you might have with your kids, and bring new ideas to your own life.

Conversation Starters

1. What is your earliest money memory?

2. How are your money values the same or different from those of your parents?

3. How do you discuss and handle finances with your spouse?

4. What are your financial goals?

5. What lessons are you trying to teach your kids about money?

6. What conversations are you having about money with your parents?

7. What is the best financial advice that you have received?

8. What does financial independence look like for you?

A Conversation with Your Advisors

Money is about much more than dollars and cents. It's about our family, it's about our first experiences with money, it's about our life values, and it's about the conversations we do or do not have with the people who influence our saving, investing, sharing, and spending. These conversations are key, but they don't always turn into "big conversations" because money remains a taboo subject. My job is to help my clients to have these conversations so they can make the best financial decisions, decisions that align with their goals *and* their values.

I love what I do and my favorite days are when clients explicitly explain how these conversations have helped them. For example, after a difficult divorce, one client thanked me for helping her let go of the pieces of her divorce that were preventing her from making future financial decisions. She said, "I felt a lightness about the whole situation and feel like I've moved through some of the resentment and anger I was struggling with. You really helped me get to that place."

My goal is always to get to know who my clients are and how they think about money both individually and as a couple. Without this intimate knowledge, it's impossible to develop a financial plan that goes beyond dollars and cents and fits their personal needs and wants. The following steps are the most effective ways to find a financial advisor who will provide a personal touch.

1. LOOK FOR AN ADVISOR WHO ADDRESSES YOUR GOALS AND VALUES.

Arguably the most important (and perhaps the most overlooked) part of the financial planning process is the method by which defined goals are brought into focus. A clear path for achieving goals should be set, values should be talked about during that conversation, and a plan should be put into place to follow that path. As we've discussed in this book, there is much more to financial management than pure ROI (return on investment). How will your decisions affect your lifestyle, your family's future, your relationship with your spouse? There is an emotional and lifestyle component to financial management that cannot be overlooked in favor of a pure ROI approach. Holistic, goals-based financial planning requires that your goals and values align. It also requires a keen understanding of the implications that taxes, Social Security, portfolio rebalancing, and asset allocation can have on your long-term plan and goals.

2. IDENTIFY AN ADVISOR WHO IS FOCUSED ON SUPPORTING YOU.

It's human nature to react when we are scared, excited, or moved by an experience. This creates the tendency to react quickly or overreact when there are disruptions—both large and small—in the financial markets. Having a relationship built on trust with a fiduciary whose expertise is rooted in not reacting emotionally to market shifts can help you stay on track with your investment goals through good times and bad.

3. FIND AN ADVISOR WHO UNDERSTANDS TRANSITIONS AND HOW THEY AFFECT FINANCIAL DECISIONS.

A trusted financial advisor harbors the practical expertise and the strategic partnerships necessary to facilitate smooth transitions during difficult life situations. This professional should have the education and resources available to evaluate and decide between different choices with quantitative and qualitative outcomes.

4. COMMIT TO FINDING A FIDUCIARY.

Fiduciaries commit to putting their clients' best interests first at all times. They operate under a code of ethics that doesn't apply to advisors who are not fiduciaries. Fiduciary advisors fully disclose how they are compensated and flag any conflict, or potential conflict, that might prevent them from working with a client. The National Association of Personal Financial Advisors (NAPFA) is the country's leading professional association of fee-only financial advisors— highly trained professionals who are committed to working in the best interests of those they serve. Their website (napfa.org) offers a tool to search for planners who meet this requirement.

These four guideposts will help you find a financial advisor who will compassionately develop and manage your financial goals.

After her sophomore year of college, our daughter, Maddy, interned at Flourish for a summer. At the end of the summer, she said, "My biggest takeaway is that financial planning is different for every client. It changes based on who they are, what they bring to the table, their financial knowledge and resources, and their history and values."

This was a heartwarming moment for me because not only

did Maddy enjoy her time working with us, but her comments also validated that Flourish is doing exactly what we set out to do. We use our tools and resources to create a holistic experience for each and every client. We create a neutral, comfortable space where our clients feel safe having tough conversations about money. We help everyone in the room find their voice and facilitate conversations that bring everyone together so we can provide an outcome that suits the needs, matches the values, and achieves the goals of all our clients.

I appreciate the opportunity to share my thoughts about money, conversations, and life experiences. The chance to introduce or explore these topics has been a true privilege. I hope you are able to use some of these lessons to flourish while exploring the path to success in your own life.

Values List[60]

1. Abundance	24. Connection	46. Expertise
2. Achievement	25. Consciousness	47. Expressiveness
3. Activism	26. Conservation	48. Fairness
4. Adventure	27. Contentment	49. Faith
5. Affluence	28. Contribution	50. Fame
6. Ambition	29. Control	51. Family
7. Approval	30. Cooperation	52. Financial
8. Art(s)	31. Country	independence
9. Authenticity	32. Creativity	53. Fitness
10. Beautiful things	33. Decisiveness	54. Flexibility
11. Beauty	34. Devotion	55. Forward-looking
12. Belonging	35. Dignity	56. Freedom
13. Challenges	36. Discipline	57. Friendship
14. Change	37. Diversity	58. Frugality
15. Clarity	38. Duty	59. Generosity
16. Collaboration	39. Education	60. Growth
17. Comfort	40. Enjoyment	61. Happiness
18. Commitment	40. Ecology/	62. Harmony
19. Community	Environment	63. Having the best
20. Compassion	42. Ethics	64. Health
21. Competence	43. Excellence	65. Helping others
22. Competition	44. Excitement	66. Home
23. Confidence	45. Experience	67. Honesty

---

60   List compiled by TurningPoint.

68. Imagination
69. Independence
70. Individuality
71. Influence
72. Innovative
73. Integrity
74. Intelligence
75. Intimacy
76. Investing
77. Joy
78. Justice
79. Kindness
80. Knowledge
81. Leadership
82. Learning
83. Listening
84. Love
85. Loyalty
86. Making a difference
87. Mastery
88. Meaningful work
89. Mindfulness
90. Money
91. Nature
92. Open-mindedness

93. Order
94. Originality
95. Owning
96. Peace
97. Perfection
98. Philanthropy
99. Play
100. Pleasure
101. Power
102. Privacy
103. Productivity
104. Prosperity
105. Purpose
106. Reason
107. Recognition
108. Recreation
109. Relationships
110. Reliability
111. Religion
112. Reputation
113. Resilience
114. Resourcefulness
115. Respect
116. Responsibility
117. Safety
118. Security
119. Self-reliance
120. Sensuality

121. Serenity
122. Service
123. Significance
124. Simplicity
125. Spirituality
126. Stability
127. Status
128. Stewardship
129. Success
130. Teaching
131. Thrift
132. Thriving
133. Tradition
134. Transcendence
135. Transformation
136. Trustworthiness
137. Truth
138. Uniqueness
139. Unity
140. Virtue
141. Vision
142. Wealth
143. Wellness
144. Wisdom
145. Worthiness
146. Other

Acknowledgments

Writing *Flourish Financially* was like giving birth and adding a new member of the family. I appreciate all of my family, friends, and clients who helped move the process forward to write my first book, never losing faith in me or giving up on why this book was written. *Flourish Financially* is dedicated to my three children, Maddy, Fernando, and Grace, all of whom appear in this book in one way or another. In addition, I dedicate this book to my patient and loving husband (Jay) and my incredibly encouraging parents (Bob and Diane). I thank my close friends and support group who gave me the courage to go off on my own and found Flourish Wealth Management, and my Women Presidents' Organization (WPO) and Goddesses of Financial Planning (GOFP) crew who are a crucial part of any personal and professional success I find in my journey through life. I want to thank the team at Flourish Wealth Management! I am proud of what we are building and am excited for what we can accomplish together. I thank my clients for allowing me to be a part of their lives. The relationships we've built over the years have been incredibly rewarding personally and professionally. Finally, I need to thank the dedicated team of editors, entrepreneurs, and influencers at Advantage Media Group|ForbesBooks for planting the seed that turned into this book. I am forever grateful for the journey that we traveled together.

Flourish Today

LEARN MORE ABOUT KATHY

To take Kathy's free assessment and learn how
you too can Flourish Financially visit:
www.kathylongo.com hello@kathylongo.com

WORK WITH KATHY

To take Kathy's Financial Satisfaction and
Life Transitions surveys visit:
www.flourishwealthmanagement.com
952.392.4474 info@flourishwm.com
3300 Edinborough Way, Suite 420
Edina, Minnesota 55435

CONNECT WITH KATHY

 @flourishfinancially

 Kathy Longo, CFP®, CAP®, CDFA

 @kathleen_longo